PROCESS AND RELATIONSHIP

PROCESS AND RELATIONSHIP

Issues in Theory, Philosophy,
and Religious Education

A Festschrift for Randolph Crump Miller

Edited by
IRIS V. CULLY
and
KENDIG BRUBAKER CULLY

Religious Education Press
Birmingham, Alabama

Library of Congress Cataloging in Publication Data
Main entry under title:

Process and relationship.

   Includes bibliographical references.
   Includes index.
   1. Christian education—Addresses, essays, lectures.
2. Theology—Addresses, essays, lectures. 3. Philoso-
phy—Addresses, essays, lectures. 4. Miller, Randolph
Crump, 1910-   —Addresses, essays, lectures.
I. Cully, Iris V. II. Cully, Kendig Brubaker.
III. Miller, Randolph Crump, 1910-
BV1473.P76   230   77-18760
ISBN 0-89135-012-8

34,064

Religious Education Press, Inc.
1531 Wellington Road
Birmingham, Alabama 35209
2 3 4 5 6 7 8 9 10

*Religious Education Press publishes books and educational materials exclusively
in religious education and in areas closely related to religious education. It is
committed to enhancing and professionalizing religious education through the
publication of significant scholarly and popular works.*

CONTENTS

Dedicatory Preface

Because the practitioners of religious education are many and the seminal theoreticians are few—and Randolph Crump Miller ranks at the summit of both categories—we who are his friends, colleagues, and admirers wanted to honor him by stressing aspects of theology, philosophy, and religious education which have been noteworthy emphases in his own thought. It is at the ideological level that new thrusts occur which ultimately affect practice.

These chapters are offered, then, as a tribute to Professor Miller by only a few of the scores of fellow theologians, philosophers, and religious educators who have profited by his thought or have been warmed by his rich humanity.

Lexington, Kentucky   IRIS V. CULLY
1977   KENDIG BRUBAKER CULLY

INTRODUCTION

Kendig Brubaker Cully

In a work designed to celebrate the career of a particular person it would be only natural to seek a thematic structure derived from interests, concerns, and competencies of the one being honored.

Thus it was fairly evident from the beginning of the planning of this Festschrift for Randolph Crump Miller that its contributors should be asked to address themselves to matters related to Miller's primary intellectual and pragmatic thrusts. Two in number, they are most aptly designated as process and relationship.

It was not the editors' intention to ask the writers merely to extrapolate ideas from Miller's work or to attempt to develop some of his seminal ideas even further. Rather, each contributor was requested to reflect on some aspect of process or relationship (or both) which seemed of moment in relation to the writer's own interests, concerns, or stance. Miller, it was thought, would like such an approach, since he has always encouraged others to work out their own things.

It soon became obvious that the matrix of these themes would be cross-sectional of necessity. Both process and relationship pertain to the broad reaches of theology, philosophy, and pedagogy. (One might even go so far as to say that they have implications for every angle of the human endeavor, not being limited to the three fields indicated.)

In the opening chapter, "The Problem and the Clue," Professor Iris V. Cully borrows a clue from Miller's own thought processes. Just as Miller sought in relational theology a clue to Christian education, so, presently, a clue for a theory of Christian education might be found freshly in a theology of creation. All of this, it is suggested, must be done in the realization that even a new theory must be recognized as being in process, instead of possessing the qualities of permanence or unchangeability. In such a view, each period must seek to formulate anew a theory of religious education which will take into account the gathered impact of the past on the present and the emerging future.

Dean Neely D. McCarter then proceeds into an analysis of the difficult problem as to how the field of Christian education might be organized. He examines such concepts as theory itself, objectives, knowledge, means, strategies, and organization. In a related chapter, "Ways of Knowing," Professor Sara Little essays the approach to teaching *about* teaching. She foreshadows the later chapters on process by scrutinizing the relation between subject matter and the content of process, as well as various options open for decision-making about teaching.

That content and process are not unrelated but deeply conjoined becomes the theme of Professor James Michael Lee's chapter, "Process Content in Religious Instruction." He demonstrates that "process . . . is not simply a way to achieving content: process is an authentic content." The writer explores the implications of this idea for religious instruction, arguing for the use of "substantive process content" in curriculum "in terms of specified observable performance objectives."

Part I, "Process and Communication: Aspects of Educational Philosophy and Methodology," is concluded with David R. Hunter's chapter interpreting education as "an endless ontological search." *The* process of learning for him, is "discovering and experiencing the meaning and purpose of human existence," which, to ignore or stifle, would be "to contribute to the death of the spirit."

Part II examines in considerable detail some aspects of the philosophy of process under the heading "The Pursuit of Process." It is begun with Professor Charles F. Melchert's scrutiny of the term "understanding" as that is to be viewed in religious education. Viable usages of the term are discussed, in light of the complexity of the definitional task. The process of understanding is seen as "a cognitive process of structuring experience or data." Such cognition, however, in the religious field, must entail "the kind of empathetic attitude characterized by the term 'being understanding.'"

What anthropologists have long known—that the bestowing of a name conveys a creative act, and makes a thing or person—is conceived by Professors David and Margaret Steward as constituent of the structure of the church's educational ministry. This naming is done within the context of an intentional community which is living out a tradition. They see this naming ministry as taking effect through corporate worship, ethical lifestyles, and mission in the world.

The technical understandings of process in the thought of Alfred North Whitehead are set forth in Professor Ewert H. Cousins' chapter entitled "Dialogue with Whitehead's Process God." Acknowledged as the modern chief proponent of this type of philosophical methodology, Whitehead must necessarily figure in discussions of process at any level. Cousins relates his thought not only to the view of God and the trinity, but also to the Christian mystical tradition and the emergent dialogues of Christianity with other world religions. At the same time an important historical retrospective on process thought is provided by Theodore A. McConnell in his essay on "Being and Nonbeing in Pre-Socratic Philosophy." The thought of Heraclitus, Parmenides, Anaxagoras, Democritus, and Gorgias is examined, leading into the perennial discussion within philosophy of what McConnell calls the "process idea of relationship between being and becoming."

With Part III the book moves into aspects of process theology, especially as this approach relates to "Relationships, Human and Divine." The contemporaneity of the concern is manifested in Professor Rosemary Radford Ruether's "Sexism and God-talk," which she calls "models of relationship." She projects a "vision of transformatory process," which pertains to "the reconciliation of humanity with itself; the reconciliation of people with each other, and humanity with nature." Professor Howard Grimes interprets the divine-human relationship in terms of the complementarity of process thought and developmental psychology, the latter of which he sees in terms of the Piaget-Erikson, Kohlberg-Fowler continuum.

Reuel L. Howe interprets "The Imperative Dialogue" as the necessary dialogue of persons with nature, with other persons, and with God. He sees the world as an arena for self-actualization on the part of humankind, as an arena for self-revelation on the part of God, as the sphere of mission for the church, and as the testing-ground of individuals' professions of faith. Professor Donald E. Miller speaks of "Revelation and the Life Cycle," which takes into account "the endless sequence of emerging structural possibilities" pointing toward "the underlying force that keeps both form and change in relation with each other, each immediately affecting the other." As a tool toward the implementation of this process insight, he focuses on story-telling as "central to the teaching ministry of the church."

Finally, Boardman W. Kathan writes a brief "life" of Randolph Crump Miller, showing the influences on his developing thought and career, outlining the books he has produced, and evaluating his place in American religious education during recent decades. Included also is a bibliography of Miller's writing from 1935 to early 1977.

CHAPTER 1

THE PROBLEM AND THE CLUE

Iris V. Cully

When the forthright affirmations of neo-orthodox theology met the pragmatic religious education movement (itself a reaction to an earlier orthodoxy) there might well have been an impasse. Instead there was dialogue, however uneasy, whereby some appropriation of religious education learning theory became combined with the theological-biblical views then prevalent in one sector of American-European studies.

This became possible because the first book to respond to the challenge was Randolph Crump Miller's *The Clue to Christian Education.* He interpreted theology in terms broad enough for accommodation to the process of education.

The problem had been set. How can dynamic structures of education be developed within the framework of the "givenness" in the Christian faith? The church has a history, and this past may not be neglected without peril of unbalancing the continuity with present and future. There are statements of faith, inherited from the earliest days. However broadly interpreted, some affirmations cannot be discarded without changing the meaning of Christian belief. There is a basic scripture which cannot be ignored, however much it may be neglected. These writings can come under all kinds of scrutiny: historical, literary, archeological, or psychological—but they are still basic. They are to be read and taught in the churches and by individuals, for study, meditation, liturgy, and as a guide to living. This is, in short, the word of God to those who believe. Without

This essay was presented as a substantive part of Iris V. Cully's address at her installation as Alexander Campbell Hopkins Professor of Religious Education, Lexington Theological Seminary.

1

it, Christian churches would be different. There are cultic observances: the weekly rites of word and sacrament, the once-and-for-all rite of baptismal initiation, and the rites of passage. However flexibly these may be written or conducted, they are descriptions of Christian self-understanding.

Moreover, there is the concreteness of each particular situation. Action is concrete. Being itself is concrete. One works from this statement in assessing the possibility of change.

The problem of combining concreteness and givenness with a dynamic flexible educational approach has been around a long time. Every sensitive teacher from Greek times to the present has sought to provide a balance. The answer for some is to jettison the tradition and develop new forms of faith; new affirmations, words, and liturgies. These would have only a tenuous connection with the past, but they might meet the expressed needs of people. The historic sense is not that strong among a people who trace their own history through so few centuries, nor is it so deep among Protestants who have been wont to trace their ecclesiastical history from the sixteenth century. Other Christians have a longer sense of tradition. This approach of concentrating on the present expression is newly-popular, especially in the field of liturgy and in the restatement of credal formularies into contemporary terms. Biblical reinterpretation has been around a long time—at least since the time of Origen at the end of the second century, and among the rabbis for a much longer time.

Miller's answer is to see theology and religious education as process. This is neither a combination of the given and the flexible, nor a fusion; not a compromise or choice. Nor can it be contained by Dewey's phrase, "reevaluation of values," for that implies more change than a historically-based tradition would find acceptable. A relational theology is the clue. Relationships are always dynamic, with every possibility of changing for the better. They are ongoing, and they incorporate the past while living in the present and looking toward the future. With such an approach to theology, one can also see process in education.

The answer worked for a long time. Religious educators who personally stood within a tradition that based educational practice on inherited guidelines were able to relate this to a developmental approach to persons, materials, and methods that had been important in the liberal religious education movement. They could affirm that the term "living tradition" was not a contradiction. "Living" meant a sense of interrelationships, past and present, of seeing biblical people in their particular time while recognizing that people today share the same needs and live in parallel situations. There was an existential note: the Bible speaks to each person, declaring redemption. If salvation had classically been understood as release from sin and the power of evil, now it seemed to offer release from anxiety and growth into selfhood. Later it was to become interpreted as liberation from social or economic oppression.

Can any theology be pivotal for religious education theory today? Sara Little, writing in *Foundations for Christian Education in an Era of Change*[1] answers negatively. There is no consensus among theologians, and each new approach has its day of popularity (heralded by an article in one of the newsweeklies), only to be succeeded by the next wave. There is little possibility for a religious education theory to develop around such short-lived systems. Paulo Friere, in his book *Pedagogy of the Oppressed* developed a methodology, but his framework is cultural and sociological more than it is theological. Is it possible that James Michael Lee called for an end to a theological basis for education not a moment too soon?[2]

Many still see hope in the possibility of education by incorporation into a faith community. Is there an answer that can take cognizance of the richness of biblical words and faith pronouncements? Can there be a theological restatement that would make an acceptable working basis for a religious education theory?

The circle begun with *The Clue to Christian Education* inevitably led toward a study of process theology and implications for Christian education.[3] Process thinking should have been apparent to those who read the earlier book, but readers were satisfied simply to hear that there could be a theological approach to Christian education. Now this ingredient can be clarified. To be dynamic is to be empowered—and this surely is a factor in Christian theology. To be empowered by God through his Spirit is to be in process of change. The process

theologian goes even further and sees no limitation to the being
or power of God in affirming that God also is in process of
change—always beyond that of human potential. Human beings, redeemed, are in process of change. "Behold I make all
things new" is the triumphant assertion in the closing book of the
Bible. "The new life" and "newness of life" are biblical terms.

Because life is dynamic, a way of living will also be continually
changing, however slowly. Twentieth century events have
changed many ethicists from reliance on a morality of rules to
one that is, at the least, contextual. One cannot be "honest" or
"truthful" in a vacuum. These are not theological constructs,
but lived realities.

Process is more clearly seen in educational terms, for what
else is education if not development? "Process" is one of the
most used words in the educational vocabulary. It connotes a
willingness to accept the learner and to watch development,
intervening only with great care. Growth is dynamic. Religious
development shares this dynamism. While each mode of belief
and practice is "right" for a particular age, there is continual
change in the individual understanding of and relationship to
God, and the ability to grasp the tradition in its ongoing forms.
Persons grow in the ability to make ethical decisions, and in the
kinds of influence they receive from other persons and the total
environment in such decision making.

To speak of process in theology or education is not to affirm
instability or flux. Continuous change is itself a modus oper-
andi. A religious education theory explicates why this is and
how it becomes facilitated.

God as dynamic reality works out his purposes in a world in
which people live in societies. These are organismic, developing
in many ways (Teilhard de Chardin would also add "cosmic").
The unpredictability of much human behavior, in spite of
seemingly deep attachment to habits, makes it inevitable that
change be seen as integral to personal growth. The Christian
affirmation about life has made love central: loving God and
the neighbor. This reflects an awareness that people are more
easily persuaded than threatened. Love is a powerful motivating force. This is the theme of *The Spirit and the Forms of Love* by

Daniel Day Williams.[4] Love always involves freedom, for it cannot be coerced. So freedom becomes a factor in this understanding of life.

Translated into educational terms, this means that people, undergirded by the loving acceptance of others in family or Christian community, may become aware of the freedom to make decisions. Given opportunities to participate through worship and service—love in action—they are enabled to develop most fully. This is an experience-centered approach to learning. It draws on the experience of the past, for each member participates in the history and example of earlier communities.

If it continues the past, it also looks toward the future. Christianity is an eschatological religion, with an openness to the future as the fulfillment of God's redeeming purposes. This is a dynamic view of the world, carrying a realization that while humans participate in this process, God is the originator. The creativity of humans is bound up in this awareness. They do not create *ex nihilo,* as it is stated in classical terms that God has created. They bring new forms from rearrangements of the materials of creation. Such new configurations constitute a process by which humans fulfill the gifts given them. Education can open up the potential for creation in art as well as in actions toward the transformation of relationships and all other areas of life.

Miller suggested a relational theology as the clue to Christian education. At the present time, a theology of creation itself may give a clue for a theory of Christian education. The continual creative work of God, the new creation in Christ, the broad-ranging power of the Holy Spirit, the changing dynamics of human relations, the ever-renewed life of the Christian community among its people and within the world, are elements in such a theory. This too will be subject to modification in the dynamic development of theology and of education, and in the expanding knowledge of the world and human beings. An educational theory is not expected to be valid for all time but is developed for its usefulness at a particular time. It too is in process.

Notes

1. Ed. Marvin J. Taylor, Abingdon Press, 1976, p. 30f.
2. *The Shape of Religious Instruction*, Religious Education Press, 1971.
3. *Religious Education*, Vol. 68, 1973, p.307f.; symposium: "Process Theology and Religious Education."
4. Cf. Daniel Day Williams, "The Spirit and the Forms of Love," Harper, 1968.

PART I

PROCESS AND COMMUNICATION: ASPECTS OF EDUCATIONAL PHILOSOPHY AND METHODOLOGY

CHAPTER 2

ORGANIZING THE FIELD OF CHRISTIAN EDUCATION

Neely Dixon McCarter

Those of us who studied with Randolph Crump Miller and have continued to work with him over the years have learned to respect his ability to relate theory and practice. His books and articles which set forth his theoretical perspectives on the field have been accompanied by curricular designs, teacher-training programs, and the like. He has stimulated theoreticians and practitioners.

Therefore, it seems appropriate to write an article which seeks to contribute to both the theory and the practice of Christian education. I wish to propose a formal organization for the field; i.e., the subject-matter of Christian education.[1] This organization, constructed formally, should be of help to teachers and practitioners of Christian education as they think about the subject, construct theory, and design specific Christian education courses and programs. I am not proposing a theory of Christian education, nor a theory of practice (though I come close to this by offering a way of organizing our field), nor a theory of the methodology of the field, though there may be implications for this in what follows.

An organization of the field presented formally provides a structure for theoretical and practical analysis and construction in very much the same way as the organization of biblical studies provides a frame of reference for persons working in that field. The categories of linguistics, historical studies, critical studies, etc., furnish a structure for the student in biblical studies without suggesting whether or not the person is working as a conservative, liberal, or whatever. The material con-

9

tent, perspectives, and outlook will vary from person to person or tradition to tradition.

Furthermore, to organize the field of Christian education does not suggest that everyone who works in the field is an expert in every area any more than a person working in biblical studies would be expected to excel in linguistics, historical studies, or the like.

Working without some organization of the field leads to the point of view expressed by Marvin J. Taylor in 1966:

> For Christian Education is really a collective discipline, catching up much of its substance from other areas (biblical and theological studies, learning theory, psychology, educational philosophy, etc.). In fact, its very diversity is so great that some even question whether it has any central unity.[2]

It seems to me to be difficult to carry on systematic, theoretical, and practical analysis and construction operating with this perspective.

I acknowledge that my efforts to organize the field formally are influenced by Sara Little, with whom I plan, think, and team-teach. When I admit that Marc Belth, Charles Melchert, R. S. Peters, Thomas Green and others have also influenced me, the reader will know at once that education is normative in my thinking about and doing Christian education. Even though Randolph Miller would argue that theology should be normative and James Michael Lee would insist upon the social sciences,[3] I believe both persons could use the formal organization of the field proposed here.

The field of Christian education can be formally organized using the following rubrics: theory, objectives, knowledge, strategies, means, and organization.

Immediately some of you are noting that there seems to be no place for the history of Christian education, theology, biblical studies, psychology, sociology, and the like. The answer to this is to suggest that these are sources which generate data which in turn are used in the theoretical and practical analyzing and constructing of both the theory and practice of Christian education. The formal organization thus allows one to "locate" readings and data from various sources; i.e., put them into some frame of reference.

To illustrate how the organization of the field formally stated can be used, I will have to become normative (i.e., material) in my assertions. The limitations of space and the writer's abilities prevent any full statement of an approach to Christian education; nevertheless, a sample of what might be done can be suggested.

Theory. Under this rubric one can deal with definitions of theory, the relation of theory to practice, and a comparison of theories.

My own reading of Peters, Belth, Melchert, and others has led me to the conviction that education is autonomous and distinctive.[4] When one thinks about education or engages in educational pursuits, one is dealing with reality from a distinctive point of view. One is raising the question of nurturing the ability to think, to use Belth's language,[5] or focusing on the cognitive, to refer to Peters;[6] or, as Thomas Green says, "... at the heart of education is the effort to enhance the human capacity to think."[7]

Working from this point of view one can draw upon many sources in understanding the cognitive domain (which is not as limited as some assume),[8] models of thinking, the development of persons and their abilities in the cognitive realm, etc.

But one should also compare this theoretical approach to that of Ellis Nelson[9] or John Westerhoff.[10] These two writers represent a socialization model of education which uses a different methodology from the one I have suggested above. Nevertheless, it is just this type of analyzing, comparing, and constructing of theory and practice that is suggested by my organizational guidelines.

Objectives. Again, one should define educational objectives, levels of objectives (goals, purposes, denominational objectives, objectives for a particular session, etc.), compare objectives from various eras, deal with the relation of objectives to content and the structure of a particular session, etc.

If one follows my theoretical position, many of the purposes and objectives stated for the Christian education enterprise will have to be ruled out. To bring another person to faith is not an educationally viable objective. To be sure, to understand the faith can be seen as a component in coming to the faith. To come to have faith may be the aim of the church, but there is no educational process, as I have defined the same, that can do this. Charles Melchert has cogently argued this case in his Yale Ph.D. dissertation, "An Exploration in the Presuppositions of Objective Formation for Contemporary Protestant Christian Education Ministry."[11]

But one must not only struggle with appropriate objectives for the field of Christian education; one must study, analyze, and learn to write objectives for local congregations, curricular pieces, and individual sessions.

Knowledge. If education is involved with the enhancing of the human capacity to think, education is dealing with knowledge. What is the knowledge with which Christian education is concerned? Further, is there a difference between the nature of biblical knowledge and theological knowledge? How is theological knowledge made and used? What type of knowledge concerned Kierkegaard and why is it important to those of us in Christian education? Does not the nature of biblical knowledge, for example, change over the generations?

In short, working in the field of Christian education involves one in the analysis of types of knowledge, persons and their ability to deal with various types of knowledge (when can a child grasp historical knowledge?), and appropriate ways of teaching the varieties of knowledge used in Christian education. Sara Little has dealt with this area in some detail in her chapter in this book. She indicates the relation of types of knowledge to the section on teaching below.

Means. This category needs at least two subdivisions; the first is teaching. Obviously the approach to teaching most congenial with my own position is the one proposed by Green in his *Activities of Teaching.* Green can be supplemented by such books as Bruce Joyce and Berj Harootunian's *The Structure of Teaching* and Joyce and Weil's *Models of Teaching.*[12] One must deal with both the theory and practice of teaching. Again, I refer you to Little's chapter for an expansion of these ideas.

The second division deals with learning resources. Here one

is involved in the analysis and use of curricula and media resources. One needs some theory of curriculum as well as the ability to design and construct learning environments.

There are many sources from which data are generated for this area, such as developmental psychology and mass communication, to say nothing of the Christian tradition.

Strategies. Flowing from the above begin to emerge some possible strategies. What overall approach or approaches should one use in carrying out the educational task of the church? Though there is a difference between education and schooling, the school strategy can be used. The parochial school, the Sunday school of the church, the mid-week school of the church, and, in our time, perhaps, the public school.[13]

The home nurture strategy has been under consideration as a formal approach at least since the time of Horace Bushnell. Perhaps there is a strategy to be found in the minority community mentality, illustrated for us by the Hebrew tradition.

There are no doubt others, but work needs to be done in the area of history as well as sociological analysis of the current scene if viable strategies for Christian education are to emerge.

Organization. Strategy implies some type of organization. How does one organize a denomination, a board or agency, a local congregation, or a particular class in order that education can best take place? Here data are generated from such diverse sources as church or denominational tradition, the organizational development movement, group process, and the like.

There are no doubt many other ways of organizing the field of Christian education. My colleague, Sara Little, and I have found this structure useful in our efforts to think about and do Christian education.

Notes

1. I am deliberately using the term *field* instead of discipline. The latter refers to a discrete selection of knowledge or area of human learning. I do not wish to become engaged in the debate as to whether or not Christian education is a discipline.
2. Marvin J. Taylor, Ed. *An Introduction to Christian Education.* Nashville: Abingdon Press, 1966, p. 5.
3. Miller's position is illustrated in this quotation: "I am convinced that an autonomous Christian Education finds its source in theology, and that

what we know of God and man in terms of Christian doctrine determines our objectives, our theory, and our method," p. viii, *Education for Christian Living*, 2d ed., Prentice-Hall, 1963. See James M. Lee, *The Shape of Religious Instruction*, Religious Education Press, 1971; *The Flow of Religious Instruction*, Religious Education Press, 1973. I am conscious of the fact that Lee draws a distinction between religious education and religious instruction. Nevertheless, I believe my statement as to the social sciences being normative for him holds true. Lee asks the question: "By asking the question: 'Does religious instruction fall within the category of natural science, mathematical science, social science, theological science, and so forth?' we will be able to more clearly ascertain the objectives, boundaries, methodology, and activities proper to religious instruction...." He answers his own question by saying: "The conclusion of this critical investigation will be that *religious instruction is a kind of social science and not a kind of theological science*." *The Shape of Religious Instruction*, pp. 98–99. (Italics his). Admittedly, Lee is only talking about instruction and not the field of Christian education.

4. See Charles F. Melchert, "The Significance of Marc Belth for Religious Education," *Religious Education*, vol. LXIV, No. 4, July–August, 1969, pp. 261–265.

5. Marc Belth, *Education as a Discipline*, Allyn & Bacon, 1965, pp. 7ff.

6. R. S. Peters, *Education as Initiation*, University of London Institute of Education, 1970.

7. Thomas E. Green, *The Activities of Teaching*, McGraw-Hill Book Co., 1971, p. 218.

8. See, e.g., Joseph Church, *Language and the Discovery of Reality*, Vintage Books, 1961.

9. C. Ellis Nelson, *Where Faith Begins*, John Knox, 1967. In an address in 1970, "Is Church Education Something Particular?" (published by the Boards of Christian Education of the United Presbyterian Church and the Presbyterian Church, U.S.) Nelson states a point of view similar to the writer's in specifying the particular nature of the educational process.

10. John H. Westerhoff, III and Given Kennedy Neville, *Generation to Generation*, Pilgrim Press, 1974.

11. Charles F. Melchert, "An Exploration in the Presuppositions of Objective Formation for Contemporary Protestant Christian Education Ministry." Yale University Ph.D. dissertation, unpublished, 1969.

12. Science Research Associates, 1967, and Prentice-Hall, 1972. There are numerous other volumes such as C. J. B. MacMillan and Thomas W. Nelson's *Concepts of Teaching: Philosophical Essays*, Rand McNally & Co., 1968, and Muska Masston's *Teaching: From Command to Discovery*, Wadsworth Publishing Co., 1972. Good books are available which deal with teaching theoretically as well as practically.

13. I am indebted to Robert W. Lynn for the term *strategies*. See his *Protestant Strategies in Education*, Association Press, 1964. My colleague, Sara Little, was the one who assisted in seeing this rubric, as well as others, in this outline.

CHAPTER 3

WAYS OF KNOWING: AN APPROACH TO TEACHING ABOUT TEACHING

Sara Little

"How far does the truth admit of being learned?" With that question, Soren Kierkegaard, speaking through the pseudonymous Johannes Climacus, begins his intriguing inquiry in *Philosophical Fragments*. It is a question which all serious teachers ask at one point or another. Kierkegaard picked up the concern from Plato's *Meno*, saying that Socrates had gone as far as human reason could go in achieving an answer, but that he had neglected to consider other ways of knowing than the rational, ways possibly presupposing or leading to different understandings of the nature of truth.

Possibilities for thinking about teaching present themselves immediately. What are those other ways of knowing? What types of knowledge exist? Then one thinks about another comment of Kierkegaard's. He refers to Socrates' "wonderful consistency" in his assuming the role of midwife and thus "through his manner of living giving artistic expression to what he had understood."[1] How is Socrates' maieutic approach consistent with his belief in the power of reason? Is the way one would teach one type of knowledge different from the teaching of another type? Does the methodology flow from the subject-matter of a particular kind of knowledge? Or is method a neutral set of skills to be employed as appropriate across categories of types of knowledge?

Theoretical questions, yes. But in the final analysis, they are also quite practical questions. At least, that has proved to be the

case as they have been considered in teaching seminars worked
out at Union Theological Seminary in Richmond by Dean
Neely McCarter and myself.[2] Because the approach has been
productive, and because it is still in process—perhaps eventually to be developed into a more technical analysis of models of
knowledge—it is presented here as stimulus to the thinking of
others and as an invitation for response. Further, because of
the high importance attached to process, it is offered in honor
of Randolph Crump Miller. Note, however, that this approach
to teaching is not developed from a process theology base. On
the other hand, it does seem to be consistent with Miller's educational theory—his view that method and subject-matter are
integrally related. What is to be learned is translated through
appropriate methods into experience where it is reflected on or
"understood" and appropriated. For Miller, theology is "the-
truth-about-God-in-relation-to-man." That theology is both
experienced truth and formulated truth. The two must occur
with consistency if learning is to take place and change is to be
effected. In other words, although the categories used are different, the intent of Miller's theory seems to be in harmony with
the approach to teaching explicated here.

THE APPROACH DESCRIBED

Questions like the ones raised thus far have given rise to an
approach to teaching which centers on analysis of a theoretical
essay to ascertain the type of knowledge being considered, and
then to use the methodology (a term used comprehensively to
include strategy, techniques, attitudes) either explicitly or im-
plicitly flowing from the type of knowledge. That is to say,
seminarians are assigned an essay. They are to teach it by a
procedure consistent with the subject-matter being presented.
For example, the Socratic method would be appropriate for the
Meno rather than a lecture about the content. Encounter with
art would be appropriate for Jerome Bruner's "Art as a Mode
of Knowing," rather than art criticism or discussion of the essay. One hour is given to teaching a peer group. The second
hour is an evaluation session led by the professor.
An illustration may help. Take the assignment to teach the

methodology implicit in Kierkegaard's *Philosophical Fragments*. A group of ten or twelve class members enter a room arranged with a row of chairs facing the windows, looking out into the trees and sunlight. One person, the teacher, speaking from behind the group, tells a story, dramatically, a story she has written. Plato's myth of the cave obviously has sparked the idea, but adaptations make it easier to enter at any one of many levels of awareness of the meaning of the Christian pilgrimage. At the end, people sit in silence for a period of time. Then the class is ended.

In the evaluation period, it becomes clear that the indirect communication[3] of which Kierkegaard speaks had been used effectively, that persons had been drawn into a searching for "the truth for *me*," in the kind of subjectivity that was nearer a faith response than a reasoned analysis of an argument could be. Since the *Meno* was studied in the preceding session, and since *Philosophical Fragments*, according to Kierkegaard, picks up where Socrates left off, considerable time is spent in comparing the two writings—the difference in kinds of knowledge being considered, the difference in the role of the teacher. What about the role of reason in each case? The nature of truth? When we begin to consider the communication of the Christian faith, what is the function of rational knowledge? Is the Socratic methodology the best for that kind of knowledge? For what age group or developmental stage is this methodology appropriate? Where does Kierkegaardian subjectivity fit in? How does one include that kind of knowledge in the church's teaching ministry?

Much of the time is spent in the consideration of such philosophical questions. But teaching skills are not ignored. What were the objectives of the session? Were the teaching strategies selected appropriately and employed with skill? Was the learning environment conducive to accomplishment of the objectives? (For example, was the row of chairs "right" for the story? Was the silence appropriate?). When the Socratic method is employed, attention is given to the phrasing of questions. The intention is to deal with skills in context. If students wish to perfect skills, other opportunities such as workshops, courses, and programmed instruction are available.

THE SELECTION OF METHODOLOGIES

Out of the various essays which have been used, seven have been selected to illustrate a variety of types of knowledge of special significance to the Christian faith. They are Jerome Bruner's "Act of Discovery" and "Art as a Mode of Knowing" in *On Knowing,* Plato's *Meno,* Kierkegaard's *Philosophical Fragments,* Martin Buber's "Education" in *Between Man and Man,* John Dewey's *Experience and Education,* and Paulo Freire's *Pedagogy of the Oppressed.* The chart on the next page, worked out by the professors,[4] offers a useful classification scheme.

The chart has been used several times, in different ways. For example, it has been used as part of an overall inductive course strategy, where students worked out their own responses to questions for each category as the course progressed; the chart was simply the professors' "homework." It has also been used in an overall deductive strategy, where the chart was given out the first day, and each session became an exploration of one methodology. There are advantages and disadvantages to each approach. The important point, however, is that a system of conceptualizing is a great help to thinking about teaching. Moreover, it promotes in persons a recognition that there is more than one way of knowing, and thus more than one way of teaching.

ASSUMPTIONS

Against the background of this overly-brief description, four assumptions may make clearer the rationale for the approach.

The content of subject-matter and the content of process must be consonant with each other if maximum learning is to occur.

David Swenson once said, "It is no slight tribute to the noble simplicity of William James as a thinker, that he put in practice so large a measure of what he had learned to understand, and actually taught pragmatism in a pragmatic manner."[5] That quotation is an interpretation of the assumption.

The Russian philosopher Nicolas Berdyaev put the matter even more forcefully when he said:

It may actually be said that in a sense "the means" which a man uses

Essay	Focal Question	Type of Knowledge	Purpose	Method	Role of Teacher
1. Act of Discovery	Can you figure this out?	Rational	Inductive thinking process—imposing structure on knowledge—learning to learn	Problem-solving	Sparks curiosity by setting problem; sequences steps of inquiry; assists students in formulating generalizations and applications
2. Meno	How can a person be altered?	Rational	Deductive reasoning—concept formation and application	Socratic	Makes sure students know he/she does not know; leads thinking by asking questions; does not give answers; has clear goal toward which to move
3. Philosophical fragments	Can you know God by means of reasoning?	Subjectivity	Self-examination—introspection—ultimately an encounter with Truth	Indirect	Refuses to enter rational argument; uses myths, parables, poems, etc., to point the student indirectly toward Truth; the processes of self-examination and making a decision are more important than content per se
4. Between man & man	Will you include me?	Any type	To nurture inclusion in a context of mutuality	Dialogical	Select from the world worthwhile knowledge; personify this knowledge; allow for individual expression or reaction
5. Experience & education	Where are you now & where do you want to go?	Experimental	To analyze & solve social problems by scientific methodology & democratic action	Laboratory—problem-solving	Be familiar with students' lives & the subject-matter; formulate the social problem and hypothesize with students; develop plans and test; evaluate in light of consequences
6. Art	What do I sense?	A-rational	Symphonic awareness; experiencing the communication	Encounter with art form	Provide appropriate art forms; give students freedom to respond
7. Pedagogy	How do I name the world?	Conative	Self-conscious and intentional action; responsible self	Problem-posing dialogue; conscientization	Analysis of situation & students' awareness; determination of generative themes; coded existential situation in problem-posing form; decode with students; list possibilities; action

are far more important than "the ends" which he pursues, for they
express more truly what his spirit is. If a man strives for freedom by
means of tyranny, for love by means of hatred, for brotherhood by
means of dissension, for truth by means of falsity, his lofty aim is
not likely to make our judgment of him more lenient. I actually
believe that a man who worked for the cause of tyranny, hatred,
falsity, and dissension by means of freedom, love, truthfulness, and
brotherhood, would be the better man of the two.[6]

Although he couches his argument in a means–ends terminol-
ogy, Berdyaev is portraying a way of knowing which ties together doctrine, spirit, and method. That is the central concern
addressed in the approach described here.

Teaching about Teaching Should Involve Both Theory and Practice.

If it is true that there is a content to the process of teaching,
and that what is understood must be translated into appropriate methodology in order to verify and internalize the
understanding, then the first assumption leads automatically to
the second. Theory and practice must go together. In fact,
when a person seeks to embody or translate a particular kind of
knowledge into a methodology, the interdependence of theory
and practice is obvious. More important, one learns to think
about the theory implicit in any teaching situation.

*A Person Internalizes More about Teaching When He or She Actually
Practices Translating a Type of Knowledge into Appropriate
Methodology Than When Knowledge is Approached in the Abstract*

What is under consideration here is the learning style utilized
by the professors. Just as students are encouraged to make their
own value judgments about approaches to teaching, so the professors have deliberately chosen a participatory, experiential,
reflective style. It is appropriate for the objectives of the course,
but it is also preferred by the professors. One important point
should be mentioned. This is not a "learning by doing" approach. John Dewey and H. Richard Niebuhr (among others)
would agree that reflection is inextricably involved in doing if
learning is to take place. Involvement and responsibility are
more important than "doing" in the learning–teaching style in
use here.

If Various Ways of Knowing Exist, Then a Person Should Become Aware of Some of the Options Open in Decision-making about Teaching.

A basic seminar in teaching, in theological education, should introduce students to theoretical options. The approach described here seems to do that. What is the difference between the rational knowledge Plato describes and that which Jerome Bruner seeks through his inquiry methodology? What role has reason played in the process of "traditioning"? If one were to exclude rational knowledge from the communication of Christian faith, what would happen? What does Martin Buber's principle of inclusion, his "seeing things from the other side," have to do with the possibility of learning? Such questions as these inevitably arise in the comparison of different positions.

In fact, when one reflects on ways of knowing in relation to the communication of the gospel, it is evident that each "way" has its unique function, and its own potential. And the learner–teacher, with a certain humility, is called to move out with a heuristic approach as decisions are made about teaching.

This approach to teaching about teaching, highly structured and carefully sequenced though it may be, *does* seem to point to the importance of process in educational theory. In that sense, it may appropriately be included in this section of essays relating to the work of Randolph Crump Miller.

Notes

1. *Philosophical Fragments.* Princeton University Press, 1936. Trans. by David F. Swenson, p. 6.
2. My report here is actually about a "project of thought"—and of teaching—that belongs to both of us, and has come out of a thinking-together process that is mutually stimulating and supportive.
3. For a technical interpretation of what is meant by "indirect communication," see Raymond E. Anderson, "Kierkegaard's Theory of Communication," *Speech Monographs*, vol XXX, no. 1.
4. I must admit that the imaginative insight evidenced in all the "focal questions" originated with Neely McCarter.
5. *Something About Kierkegaard* (rev. ed.), Augsburg Publishing House, 1941, p. 139.
6. *The Destiny of Man*, Geoffrey Bles, 1937, p. 80.

CHAPTER 4

PROCESS CONTENT IN RELIGIOUS INSTRUCTION

James Michael Lee

Throughout the history of religious instruction a duality has typically been posited between content and method. Content was long regarded as *what* is taught; as, e.g., the knowledge that there are three persons in the trinity or that the Bible is the revealed word of God. Method was considered to be *how* the content is taught; as e.g., lecturing or telling stories. Since 1950 or so there has developed a growing awareness among religious educationists that this alleged duality between content and method is nonexistent.[1] However, most of the arguments brought against the old duality have not been convincing because they have failed to address the fundamental error of the alleged duality. The fundamental error is precisely this: content and method are not and cannot be opposed or different because method is a content. Method is a form of process, and process is a full-fledged content in its own right. Unless religious educationists and educators realize this all-important fact, they will never accord to process its proper due, and as a result they will seriously weaken the effectiveness of the religious instruction act.

Process, then, is not simply a way to achieving content: process is itself an authentic content. The act of loving is a process, and this is a content. Chewing food is a process, and the stomach knows full well the effects of the absence of this kind of content. The Catholic church goes so far as to declare that certain sacraments are null or invalid when there is some serious defect or irregularity in the process by which the attempt was made to bring them into being. As there can be no sacra-

mental content without process content, as there can be no love
without process content, so too there can be no religious instructional content without process content.

As I observe in *The Content of Religious Instruction,* there are
two basic contents in all of life, and in religious instruction also.[2]
These two contents are structural content and substantive content. *Structural content* refers to the way in which the content is
brought into activity and sustained in its activity. The transmis-
sion strategy of teaching and the structured-learning-situation
strategy offer two representative examples of structural content. In *The Flow of Religious Instruction* I identify five kinds of
structural content which I place in a taxonomy proceeding
from the most general to the most specific: style, strategy,
method, technique, and step.[3] *Substantive content* refers to the
form in which the content appears. In *The Content of Religious
Instruction* I identify eight kinds of separate but highly interactive substantive contents in religious instruction: product con-
tent, process content, cognitive content, affective content, verbal content, nonverbal content, unconscious content, and lifestyle content. Each of the structural and substantive subcontents
is a genuine content in its own right. For example, the particular pedagogical technique a religion teacher employs will yield
outcomes different from those of another technique he might
have chosen. Also, the affective dimension of the substantive
content being taught will do much to shape the nature and
force of the outcome being acquired.

In religious instruction the structural content is pedagogical
procedure, while the substantive content is religion—religion as
it is given definite shape by the substance and valence of its
eight constituent subcontents. (It is the valence and configura-
tion of the eight constitutive subcontents which make religions
differ substantively among themselves.) To regard pedagogical
procedure as structural *content* represents a quantum leap toward
properly understanding and appreciating that which the old
content-method dualists myopically viewed as method.

I have introduced this consideration of structural content
and substantive content in order that a clearer and more
nuanced awareness of the nature of process content can
emerge. Unlike any of the other subcontents, process content is

a type of structural content and also a type of substantive content. This point is crucial to bear in mind, because most religious educationists and educators seem to regard process as totally an aspect of pedagogical procedure, thus failing to see that it is a mode of substantive content as well. Indeed, process content is a very important and crucial variety of substantive content. Let me use an example from arithmetic to illustrate my point. In arithmetic, it is not a sufficient learning outcome to merely know that two times two equals four. It is also important, and indeed more important, to know how two times two can be said to equal four. This process is an important content of arithmetic because it is a content in its own right. Multiply*ing* is a process content. Multiplying is an essential content of arithmetic.

Let us see how this notion of process content as a mode of substantive content applies to three substantive contents which most religious educationists and educators would readily admit are among the most important for their work: life, theology, and education.

A fundamental feature of life is experience, for life in some ways can be considered as a set of experiences. But the act of experiencing is a process content. Experience therefore has process content injected into its very makeup as a vital and essential form.

One of the great substantive contents of theology is the trinity. According to the traditional theory on the trinity, the Holy Spirit is the love which the Father gives to the Son and which the Son gives to the Father. This mutual giving and receiving is, by definition, a process. Put in other terms, the process content of the Father's and the Son's mutual love is the Holy Spirit. The third person of the trinity is defined (or perhaps more accurately, described) by classical theology as basically, though by no means totally, a process content.

The acquir*ing* of religious knowledge, the feel*ing* of Christian attitudes, liv*ing* of a Christian lifestyle are crucial to the substantive content of religious instruction. Now these are all process contents, process contents without which there could be no substantive content.

As I mentioned earlier, the overall substantive content of

religious instruction is religion. But what is religion if it is not a process—a process of living a certain kind of lifestyle? Religion is Christian lifestyle in action; it is actualizing the new person received at baptism. Religion is a process of behaving Christianly. Process content lies at the root of religion.

In religious instruction the relationship of process content and product content is one of intimacy, complementarity, and tension. Process and product are closely interwoven, for every product is in process and every process is conjoined to a (processing) content. Process and product are complementary because each encompasses one of the two great realities of life, change and permanence. Process and product exhibit the same inbuilt but fruitful tension as any other expression of becoming and being.

"Product content is something that has been performed in the sense of a completed process; process content is something which is being performed."[4] To borrow a conceptualization from Gilbert Ryle, product content is "knowing *that*," and process content is "knowing *how*."[5] In religious instruction for example, knowing that racial discrimination is un-Christian constitutes a product content. Knowing the means by which the church reached this conclusion is a process content; so also is knowing how to combat racial discrimination.

I must reemphasize that in the real order process content can never exist apart from or without product content. There is no product content which is not in process. Nor is there any process content which is not bound up with a product—there must always be some reality that is in process.

Thus far in this chapter, I have discussed the nature and importance of process content in religious instruction. My analysis has definite and far-reaching implications for curriculum-builders and teachers. It suggests that much more attention must be paid to both structural content and substantive process content.

Inasmuch as structural content is an authentic and rich content, it should not be demeaned or downplayed as is too often the case is so many preservice and inservice training programs. Many of these programs, notably at the master's level, have perhaps only a single so-called "methods course," a course which is more of a "Mr. Fix-it" operation in which the learners are given specific techniques or "tips" on teaching. Now if process means anything, it means generalizability and depth. Process is more vital and more useful than product since, among other things, it can be generalized. The process content of how to reach a particular moral conclusion, for example, can be generalized to a host of cases, while the product content of reaching a specific conclusion in *this* case cannot be legitimately generalized to other kinds of cases. One cannot, therefore, teach "tips" or "Mr. Fix-it" techniques which are applicable to situations other than those under present practice. One can just teach the underlying process content of which a specific technique represents only one instance. When teaching a particular technique, the generalized process of which this technique is but an instance must also be taught, lest the learner mistakenly believe that he can indeed apply this technique to all manner of instructional situations. Attention simply to teaching "tips" robs the learner of the possibility of mining the rich ore of process content, ore which is necessary for the coin of subsequent pedagogical effectiveness. I believe that structural content is downplayed, and often ravished, so frequently in teacher-training programs because the professors themselves are blind to the awareness that process is indeed a content.

Religion teachers typically wish to be known as "content-centered." But one cannot be content-centered unless one centers his pedagogical activities in structural (process)-content as well as in substantive process-content. Perhaps a brief story will illustrate my point. Some years ago, at a university in which I was then teaching, an internationally-celebrated European theologian came to give a summer course in religious instruction. One sunny morning this professor was lecturing on the importance of love in the teaching of religion. Using his softest voice-tones, he told the students how Jesus was such an effective teacher because he showed great love and understanding. The professor waxed eloquently on the beauty, the expansiveness, and the warmth of love, and how it is so terribly important for every religious educator to love his students and all those around him. During the middle of these sublime utterances, three graduate students from one of my own classes slipped quietly in to the back of the lecture hall, for I had urged them to hear the great man, at least once. After they had seated themselves, the professor put down his lecture notes, and in a loud voice redolent with negative affectivity demanded: "Who are you?" My students gave their names and stated their reason for entering the class. Then the professor shouted at them: "Out! Out of this room at once! How dare you interrupt my lecture!" And then the professor continued his lecture on the warmth and love which are the hallmark of true and effective religious instruction. Now what was the content which the students learned from that lecture? To this day, people I know who were students in that class tell me that they remember nothing of the product-content of the lecture, but that the structural (process)-content remains a vivid learning outcome for them.

If religious educationists and educators are typically blind to the tremendous importance of structural (process)-content, they are also generally not cognizant of the axiality of substantive process-content. Religion curricula and teachers place their emphasis on cognitive product-learnings such as selected biblical knowledges. But because they are so often unaware of process as a substantive content, they frequently neglect to deliberatively teach for such cognitive process outcomes as thinking biblically. One might know product content about the Bible, but unless one thinks biblically (process content), one will not be authentically educated unto the Bible. Religion curricula and teachers place their emphasis on affective product learnings such as learning the breadth and the depth of God's love for us. But because they are so unaware of process as a substantive content, they often neglect to deliberatively teach for such affective process outcomes as feeling love for God in the heart. Religion curricula and teachers place their emphasis on lifestyle product-content such as learning those sexual behaviors which should be a part of the lifestyle of every Christian. But because they are so often oblivious of process as a substantive content, they often neglect to deliberatively teach such lifestyle process-outcomes as the here-and-now living in a Christian manner with regard to sex.

Teaching involves evaluation, because without evaluation it is impossible to determine the degree to which learning took place. Evaluation does not follow teaching, nor is it in any way apart from teaching. Evaluation is an inextricable dimension of the very teaching-process itself.[6] The structural and substantive contents a teacher selects and deploys are partially determined, consciously or unconsciously, by how the teacher perceives he can and will evaluate whether the learner has acquired the desired outcome(s). Now, evaluation is far broader than marks: evaluation includes the teacher's verbal and nonverbal approval/disapproval during the lesson, the positive or negative reinforcers he uses, and so forth. It is only natural for the learner to gear his efforts toward securing a positive evaluation, whether that evaluation takes the form of a paper-and-pencil examination, an overt behavior test, or a reaction by the teacher during the lesson. Learning tasks are teleological—they inherently are targeted toward evaluative feedback. Thus, if process-content is to gain its due salience and potency it must be made a vital and pervasive aspect of any evaluative mode employed by the teacher or by the learner. If a teacher consciously and continuously evaluates the effectiveness of his instruction on the basis of the skilfulness of the structural content he deploys during the lesson and on the basis of the degree to which the learner has acquired the desired substantive process-contents, then we can be reasonably sure that he will suffuse the lesson with process content.[7]

In evaluating the structural content which the teacher employs, the procedure of behavioral analysis and behavioral control is eminently useful. In the first phase of this two-phased operation, the teacher analyzes his own pedagogical behavior in terms of what he sees happening in that antecedent-consequent chaining which is called human communication. Teaching, like any other form of communication, is a chained set of antecedent-consequent behaviors. For example, the teacher makes a pedagogical move (antecedent behavior). The learner responds (consequent behavior). The learner's consequent behavior then becomes an antecedent behavior for the teacher; namely, a behavior to which the teacher must respond. And so the chain continues. Now behavior is a process, a process involving different activities. By using behavioral analysis, the teacher diagnoses the process of instruction. In this analysis, breakdowns or defects in the process of facilitation are laid bare. In the second phase of this two-phased operation the teacher controls his own pedagogical behavior. He harnesses and channels his antecedent and consequent instructional moves so that they are more effective in facilitating the desired consequent learner moves.

What is stated in the previous paragraph is the very essence of teaching. If religion teachers are truly desirous of improving the structural content of their lessons, they should go to a teacher-performance center equipped with videotape recorders, microteaching laboratories, and interaction-analysis specialists. In such a teacher performance center the teacher will be immersed in process-on-the-hoof, and come to enrich his own understanding of and skill in process content.

In writing the objectives for the lesson, unit, or course, the religion teacher should make sure that he includes a goodly amount of process objectives. These objectives should be stated in performance terms, that is, the specific activity which the learner must successfully negotiate to a specified level of observable competence. Only when substantive process-content is consciously written into the curriculum in terms of specified observable performance objectives will there be any reasonable likelihood that this form of content will be consciously and successfully taught.[8]

There is much talk in both Catholic and Protestant circles about the necessity of building and enhancing community. But community is basically a process-content. It is an interactive, cohesive, caring process which characterizes a community. Community is a learned set of behaviors; put another way, it is a set of behaviors which has been taught and can be taught. In terms of structural content, community is a process which must be facilitated with ever-increasing levels of effectiveness, lest the community wither and die. In terms of substantive content, community is fundamentally a process of honest involvement, open sharing, and loving concern. If genuine community is so rare in Christian circles today it is largely because the persons who want to build and enhance community have, by and large, neglected or denigrated process content. To build and enhance community is a major objective of religious instruction. Unless process content, both structural and substantive, is recognized, felt, and actualized in the lesson, in the parsonage, and in the religious order, community will never come about.

Notes

1. See, for example, Gabriel Moran, "The Adult in Religious Education," in *Continuum*, VII (Autumn, 1969), pp. 7–9.
2. The entire third chapter of *The Content of Religious Instruction* is devoted to process-content. That chapter, as far as I know, is the first attempt in religious education literature to discuss religious instruction process as content and to treat the topic in any degree or breadth. James Michael Lee, *The Content of Religious Instruction*, Religious Education Press, to be published in 1979.
3. James Michael Lee, *The Flow of Religious Instruction*, Religious Education Press, 1973, pp. 34–35.
4. James Michael Lee, *The Content of Religious Instruction*, Chapter 3.
5. Gilbert Ryle, *The Concept of Mind*, Hutchinson, 1949, pp. 27–32.
6. On this point, see Harold William Burgess, *An Invitation to Religious Education*, Religious Education Press, 1975, pp. 158–159.
7. For a rather thorough treatment of evaluation in the educational process, see Benjamin S. Bloom, J. Thomas Hastings, and George F. Madaus, *Handbook on Formative and Summative Evaluation of Student Learning*, McGraw-Hill, 1971.
8. See Robert F. Mager, *Preparing Instructional Objectives*, Fearon, 1962.

CHAPTER 5

EDUCATION: AN ENDLESS ONTOLOGICAL SEARCH

David R. Hunter

Education is the process of discovering and experiencing the meaning and purpose of human existence.[1] From the earliest disorganized reaching out of the child to explore what is closely at hand to the creativity of the mature poet and the hypothesizing of the research scientist, the quest for meaning and purpose is basic and inescapable. The two queries, *What* and *Why*, are always before us, goading us on. When we cease to feel and respond to this pull, we have died even though we continue to live. Education is our reaching out to understand and to know life.

We are speaking, of course, from the perspective of the learner, from the orientation of the person who in one way or another is asking the question. What the educator does may or may not significantly facilitate this process. But we will return to the educator after further identifying the nature of education as it occurs within the life of the learner.

The child reaches out with curiosity first with eyes that can scarcely focus, then with fingers that can barely grasp, ears that respond to every sound within range and a mouth that sucks and takes in anything accessible. The earliest cognitive functions of the self have every appearance of being automatic and innate.[2] There is the hunger motivation and the need for affection underlying much early behavior, but when food and love are at least in fair supply, a child's wakeful hours are spent in everlasting exploration of the immediate environment, including the stuff of one's own body, its folds and appendages. Everything is new and strange, and it all becomes increasingly mystifying as the child grows in awareness and discernment. Perhaps only a precocious child would go around asking about the meaning of life per se, but all young children, precocious or not, find their own way of putting the question and continuing to ask it until it is answered or they are squelched. "What does that mean, Mommy?" This is the repetitive ontological question in nascent form. Not that a child is a small grown-up, for the child has a unique logical structure and method of functioning, but it is a structure and method which has its own coherence although always subject to contingent circumstances.[3]

Initially the child's question is completely objective, having to do entirely with what is outside the one who asks it. Gradually it comes to include the meaning the exterior object or person has for the child. When this occurs it is the dawn of self-awareness and the beginning of the consciousness-raising process which can be the threshold to incalculable suffering and joy in the years ahead.[4]

It is no wonder then that most children, once they are past the fear of being swallowed up in their first kindergarten or school, take to their early years of education with such zest. Whatever the quality of the school, it feeds their deep desire to know what life is all about. Eventually, lack of quality can put a blight on formal education, but the young child will make a rose out of the saddest weed the teacher has to offer until such time as meaninglessness finally triumphs and the child's interest turns elsewhere.

In this sense there is no difference in principle between secular and religious education. Both exist to feed the initially insatiable desire of the student to discover the meaning and purpose of the world and all that it contains. Secular education makes certain choices and establishes certain limits in determining what areas of experience the child will be permitted to explore. Religious education sometimes claims to set no limits, a rather specious claim, but, unlike secular education, it does not rule out the exploration of the spiritual and transcendental aspects of human experience. It is more likely to err in the direction of confining the scope to the spiritual or making all else subservient to it.

The great tragedy of so much organized education, however,

is the tremendous gulf and discontinuity which exists between the ongoing (sometimes blocked) process of searching in the lives of people and the programs of secular and religious education which are offered by society to meet educational needs. Both the process of searching and the program of education are important in that each pertains to matters of substantial significance, but the important question is whether they are of the same genre, whether they have much likelihood of coming together in any kind of fusion.

Part of our problem is in the fact that the education of a person (discovering and experiencing the meaning of being) is a pulsing, living, always moving process, whereas a program of education is an organized series of exposures to or confrontations with experiences and issues as someone else has known them. These two kinds of education need not be unrelated, but normally they do not coalesce for the reason that one is always a living process while the other is not necessarily so. Nor is the relationship factor enhanced by the fact that the organizing principle for the educational event usually is determined by the program and not by the living process of the learner.

Many, perhaps most, secular and religious schools have a curriculum calling for certain subjects, problems, and issues to be dealt with at specific age levels or in particular grades. The decisions concerning when and where these issues will be scheduled grow out of someone's experience or research concerning the national norm.

This norm may or may not be based on data pertaining to the real-life questions being asked by people. In any case, the materials are published on the assumption that people of a certain age throughout the whole nation, this year and until the course is revised, will be nurtured educationally by making use of them.

Is the human species so uniform, so predictable, as to permit anybody to know in what way Billy Jones and his peers will be reaching out in search of meaning at a certain year in their life in the midst of a new and constantly changing environment? Is it possible for the organizing principle of an educational program to be more closely related to the educational process currently in progress in the life of Billy Jones? If one is really concerned about such a possibility, there are ways of bringing this to pass.

In the spring of 1976, after eight years of study and research, a new curriculum of the Lutheran Church in America offered a custom-designed program which begins where a given congregation and a particular class may be. The congregation supplies essential information about the class and the local situation. The headquarters becomes a resource bank with a wealth of options which relate to the inescapable life-involvements of children, youth, and adults, and the local church leadership then has its choice of a variety of recommended options. An ongoing evaluation leads to new priorities and, as necessary, new customized resources from the denominational center.[5]

How the Lutherans and others will use this new curriculum remains to be seen, but it offers an opportunity to put the child's life-situation sharply in focus. If the data-gathering process is taken lightly or in relation to relatively insignificant questions, then this program could be as superficial in relating to an individual's search for the meaning of life as a box of bandaids would be to a hemophilia patient. The outcome will depend on whether leadership insists on focusing upon the ontological search, the search for meaning, or whether it settles for something less.

Two decades ago another denominational curriculum was built on the assumption that the organizing principle of any educational program is the crux of the matter and that fundamentally there are only two choices. A given educational course receives its direction either from what is happening in the lives of the students or from what has already happened in the minds of an editorial board. The choice is between living issues (alive now in the life of the learner) and traditional subject-matter. Note that the choice is not whether living issues or subject-matter will be used. The choice pertains to which will be in the driver's seat as the course proceeds from week to week.

This particular curriculum of the Episcopal Church took religious issues as its organizing principle and proceeded to identify the particular manifestations of a specific religious issue that are sufficiently common at a given age level to warrant making preparation for dealing with them.

An attempt was then made to provide the teacher with sufficient assistance in observing and recognizing the manifestations to permit these live issues to become the focus around which weekly plans could be made and the necessary resources selected.

It was recognized that a program such as this depended upon careful teacher training and supervision, and resources for such training were provided. Use of the curriculum was a fulfilling experience when care was taken to provide leaders who were ready and desirous of putting the living situation first. When this did not occur frustrating failure ensued.[6]

But we need to face the fact that the organizing principle at the heart of an educational program is usually dictated by personal and political allegiances—sometimes secular, sometimes religious. We use the education system to perpetuate what we favor and desire. We do so through our attachment to dominant economic and social values in both capitalist and communistic structures. The gulf and discontinuity between the quest of the learner and the content of the curriculum can be caused by the use of the curriculum as a political or special-interest tool.[7] We are also capable of doing the same through our personal devotion to a body of belief and practice which is the basis of our faith. Whether we have the right and obligation to bear such witness is not the issue. We do. The issue is whether there will be any engagement with the seeking mind and soul of the learner.

No responsible teacher or parent should withhold any conviction about reality from participants in an educational process when the conviction is germane to the questioning attitude of the participants—but the organizing principle should be the questioning attitude of the learner, not the ardent desire of the teacher. Better yet, the organizing principle should be the questioning attitude of learner and teacher, for if the teacher does not also have the expectancy to learn there will not be much of a meeting with the younger learner.

This is especially so for those who believe that all humankind is caught up in a cosmic design, the reality of which can only be experienced, never really communicated by explanation; a cosmic reality which is constantly tugging at our being, waiting and working for our response; a truth about life which alone begins to make sense out of the nonsense that threatens to envelop us, but a truth which only does so as we engage with it.

One particularly promising example of an educational program focusing on a living and central truth at the heart of community existence is the *Shalom Curriculum* spearheaded by the United Church of Christ Board for Homeland Ministries.[8] It is addressed especially to the congregation's life and lifestyle. The central theological and educational focus is the fact of shalom as a gift from God available in community—shalom in its full biblical sense—an experience of unity, well-being, community, justice, and peace. The marks of shalom and the marks of antishalom to be found currently in the life of the parish provide guidelines for the directions to be taken by organized parish life. Much depends upon the way in which worship and celebration are permitted to become the instruments of shalom reaching into every encounter and relationship in the parish.

This particular curriculum leans heavily upon the work of Jean Piaget, Lawrence Kohlberg, and Judith Torney in enabling its recommendations to relate to the most common developmental factors at various age-levels. From infancy through adulthood, the focus is on what is happening now. The past and the future find their place within the context of the emergent present.

So, as is true so often, if we are to fathom the problems of education we must begin with the simple act of definition. And if we are to define what we mean by education we must first define what we understand reality to be.

What is the most important object of learning in human experience? Whatever it is, that should be the principal focus of the learning process. All other foci are justifiable only if they support or enhance the realization of this central outreach.

The very nature and aspiration of humankind point the way for us. We are a people who instinctually are looking for reality. The human species has a persistent curiosity about life, about the meaning of life and the nature of existence. This curiosity remains persistent even if it becomes sublimated by cultural forces into questions of a more pragmatic nature shorn of philosophic content. No human interest or concern could be more basic, more important, more of the essence of things. The fact of being and the process of becoming are the very foundation of human existence.[9]

As such, the process of discovering and experiencing the meaning and purpose of human existence becomes the natural and necessary channel of the learning process. To ignore it or to stifle it is to contribute to the death of the spirit. To relate to it is to tap into the closest contact humanity has with reality.

The longest journey
Is the journey inwards
Of him who has chosen his destiny,
Who has started upon his quest
For the source of his being.[10]

Notes

1. Anyone who ventures to define education must acknowledge various degrees of indebtedness to the educational seers of past and present, but most of us also insist on asserting our individuality. Note how this definition differs from the following:

   "Education is a process of living and not a preparation for future living. All education proceeds by the participation of the individual in the social consciousness of the race."
   John Dewey, *My Pedagogic Creed*, A. Flanagan, 1898, p. 3.

   "Education consists in leading man, as a thinking, intelligent being, growing into self consciousness, to a pure and unsullied, conscious and free representation of the inner law of divine Unity, and in teaching him ways and means thereto."
   Friedrich Froebel, *The Education of Man*, D. Appleton and Co., 1897, p. 2.

   Christian education is "the systematic, critical examination and reconstruction of relations between persons, guided by Jesus' assumption that persons are of infinite worth, and by the hypothesis of the existence of God, the great Valuer of Persons."
   George Albert Coe, *What is Christian Education?* Charles Scribner's Sons, 1929, p. 296.

   "Education is a process whereby the accumulated wisdom of society is passed on to its members, and, at the same time, a process whereby members of a society reach out for new knowledge."
   Randolph Crump Miller, *Education for Christian Living*, Prentice-Hall, Inc., 1963, p. 39.

   While perhaps implied in all four, the one factor missing in each is an explicit pinpointing of the powerful ontological urge at the base of the educational process within the learner—the quest for the meaning and purpose of nature, life, and all existence.

2. "Cognitive processes seem, then, to be at one and the same time the outcome of organic autoregulation, reflecting its essential mechanisms, and the most highly differentiated organs of this regulation at the core of interactions with the environment, so much so that, in the case of man, these processes are being extended to the universe itself." Jean Piaget, *Biology and Knowledge,* University of Chicago Press, 1971, p. 26.

3. Jean Piaget, *Judgment and Reasoning in the Child,* Littlefield, Adams & Co., 1959, p. 200.

4. In this connection note the sections on the construction of reality in *The Psychology of the Child* by Barbel Inhelder and Jean Piaget, Basic Books, 1969, p. 13.

5. *Whatever Happened to Christian Education?* Lutheran Church in America, The Division of Educational Services, 1976.

6. David R. Hunter, *Christian Education As Engagement,* Seabury Press, 1963, pp. 32–40.

7. The official report of the Nairobi Assembly of the World Council of Churches, 1975, contained a critique of formal education which dealt with the role of power structures; e.g. "Education in too many societies is a consciously used instrument of power; designed to produce those who accept and serve the system; designed to prevent the growth of a critical consciousness which would lead people to want alternatives." (Report of Section 4, II, G).

8. *The Shalom Curriculum,* a basic outgrowth of pioneer planning in the United Church of Christ, is ecumenically serviced and promoted by six denominations through a partnership known as Joint Educational Development. See *Signs of Shalom,* Edward A. Powers, United Church Press, 1973.

9. Paul Tillich, *The Courage to Be,* Yale University Press, 1952. A scholarly, historical treatment of the search for being in the midst of anxiety, guilt and despair leading to "the courage to be as the key to being-itself." The closing sentence is: "The courage to be is rooted in the God who appears when God h; s disappeared in the anxiety of doubt."

10. Dag Hammarskjold, *Markings,* Alfred A. Knopf, 1964, p. 58.

PART II

THE PURSUIT OF PROCESS: ASPECTS OF THE PHILOSOPHY OF PROCESS

CHAPTER 6

UNDERSTANDING AND RELIGIOUS EDUCATION

Charles F. Melchert

Few would dispute that one of the purposes of religious education is that the learner attain understanding in religion. Indeed, for many, both conservative and liberal, Protestant, Catholic, or Jewish, the absence of understanding might well be evidence of the absence of effective religious education.

If that is so, it might be of value to know what we do when we understand in religion. We would then be in a better position to determine what we could do to help produce understanding in others.

Let us begin with some linguistic and conceptual observations.[1] First, note that understanding is related to, but not the same as, knowledge or knowing. Clearly, one cannot understand if one knows nothing, yet knowing something does not always constitute understanding. Knowing thousands of unrelated facts will not count as understanding a subject or object.

Second, two notions of understanding are often confused or conflated. There is a difference between understanding something (a proposition, an object, a person, a religion) and being understanding toward someone.[2] One can be an understanding person, or be understanding toward another, without at the same time having an understanding of that person's behavior. Conversely, one can understand another's behavior without at the same time being understanding toward him and his behavior. It is possible for each type of understanding to make one more ready to gain the other type of understanding about something or someone. Traditionally educators have been more concerned with understanding something than they have been with being understanding, so let us (for the moment at least) focus attention upon this process.

What do we do when we understand something? We can describe six elements of the act of understanding, though they will not necessarily occur in the sequence presented below.[3]

1. I attend, notice, see, image, hear, think, smell, touch, or sense something. Gestalt psychology has shown that I can attend to an object directly, focally, or I can "see" it as a part of the context of another object. How I "attend" can be influenced by many factors. I may see a bowl of bananas when I am hungry, and be aware of the bananas as something to consume, and ignore the bowl completely. If I am not hungry, and have just heard a discussion of aesthetic form, I may be more attentive to the bowl and fruit as form and grace, and less conscious of it as a source of stomach stuffing.

2. Sometimes as I attend I become aware of deficiency, or perplexity in my understanding of that object. I may feel I cannot make sense of it. I feel a need to grasp the object more fully, not only in a tactile sense, but also mentally, internally in my consciousness. This awareness of a lack of understanding may come either intentionally or quite by chance.

3. Such a recognition can either awaken or build upon a desire to understand. If Piaget is correct, every infant comes into this world with a desire to know and understand the world and self. The intensity of this desire varies, and it seems it can even be stamped out or lost. As I grow from infancy, I find that I attend more completely and desire to understand more fully those things and persons which I value or come to value.

4. Attending to the perplexity or deficiency, and wanting to understand more fully, a "pattern" emerges or is constructed. I see connections, relationships, which I did not see before—either within the object itself (thus increasing the depth of my understanding of the object), or in its relations with other objects (thus increasing the breadth of my understanding). This "seeing connections" cannot always be produced upon demand. It also happens in many different ways, perhaps as many ways as there are objects or subjects to understand and ways to understand them. Sometimes it happens quickly, other times it may take years of struggling with the problem. It can happen

consciously as I make one thing which I know a pattern or model of another which I know less well.[4] It can happen less consciously as an image "occurs to me" or "presents itself," thus fusing the disparate parts into a whole meaning.[5]

5. Thus, I say "I understand." This awareness of understanding is sometimes sudden, coming with the well-known flash of "insight," and the shout of "Eureka!" or it can dawn slowly and cumulatively, almost unnoticed. In any case, its presence often has a stimulating effect on the one who understands. There is a feeling of "having put something together." Understanding is fundamentally a unitive act, making things connected or whole which were not seen as such before.

6. However, that is not the end. Having achieved understanding, while completing an act or process, does not guarantee that the understanding is correct. As Lonergan has convincingly shown, one can have the experiences described above, say "I understand" with full sincerity, and still be mistaken. One can ask, legitimately, "But is it so?" The answer to the question, no matter how difficult to attain, is either a simple yes or no.[6] This is not to say that if one answers no, that it was all a hoax. Indeed, misunderstanding or mistaken understanding is itself an important part of the process of understanding ever more fully in depth and breadth.[7]

In other words, the process of understanding is a cognitive process of structuring experience or data. The nature of the structure arrived at or imposed will vary with the individual, and, more important, with the matter being understood. Piaget has made this structuring process very plain when it is a logical or scientific understanding. Yet such logical and mathematical structures, while they are capable of bringing understanding to a wide variety of data and experiences, cannot be the only modes of understanding appropriate to the human experience. There are some data and experiences to which such forms are not well suited. As both Suzanne Langer and studies of split-brain patients have independently shown, logical, sequential, and verbal modes of coding experience may not be best suited to spatial, visual, gestural, musical, or mystical modes of experiencing the world.[8] Yet each of these other types of human experience can be structured in ways appropriate to that type, and such a structure can legitimately be called a way of understanding that experience. For example, when one is "singing the blues," one may structure that deeply felt human experience, as well as communicate it effectively to others, and yet not participate in a logical operation. Similarly when one is ecstatically happy, and the whole body wants to "jump for joy," certain styles of dancing or acrobatics might help structure the experience meaningfully, as well as express or communicate it.

One of the reasons for this diversity of modes of understanding, is that there is something inherently tactile about the act of understanding. (Note that our language retains this tactile sense in the word itself—one "understands" as one "stands under"; i.e., submits oneself to the experience.) Piaget explains this tactile basis in his observations of children who express as well as create their understanding of their world without, and even prior to, their use of verbalization. The rudiments of intelligence are found in the sensory-motor period, in the actions of children as they handle their environment. We also know that in the early years the affective and the cognitive cannot be so readily discriminated; each tends to be present with the other in every act.

I would suggest here we come full circle to the distinction we noted at the beginning between the act of understanding something and being understanding. While Martin contends that the two are logically distinct (perhaps especially when seen in the context of explaining, as she does), I would suggest that this is less the case with some kinds of understanding. Understanding something is most distinct from "being understanding" in the sciences (though Polanyi would insist it is present even there). As one moves into areas such as art, moral values, music, and religion, not to mention interpersonal relationships, both Langer and Reid have shown that the feelings and attitudes implicit in that kind of understanding are much more integrally related to the understanding itself.[9] In understanding the "meaning" of a painting, one must have some personal involvement, some "feeling relationship" to be able to understand the work, and yet the understanding remains relatively objective, as contrasted with purely subjective. The same is not true, at least to the same degree, in mathematical or scientific thinking.[10]

I would contend that the same is true of interpersonal understanding and of understanding religious phenomena. It may be possible to understand many rituals and doctrines or history of a religion, but unless one has some direct sense of the awe which impels worship, or of the mystical apprehension of the relatedness of all things in the ground of being, then one has not really understood what gives driving force, importance, and ineluctibility to religious experience of most peoples.[11] One has not understood what produced the doctrines and rituals in the first place, and what keeps it alive even at the distance of centuries from its origins.

What might a teacher or religious educator do to help learners in the process of understanding described above? The following suggestions are not particularly new, nor are they intended to be exhaustive, but it may be helpful to affirm them in this context.

1. Diagnosis. Is there a discernible point at which the learner's understanding seems to fail? Sometimes people just do not attend carefully, especially when the material seems familiar. They need to be helped to see, to hear, to be attentive to certain clues which the teacher may recognize as having proved significant.

2. Often it helps to create perplexity or even confusion where there was none. Sometimes this can be done by pointing out that two affirmations the learner holds to be so are incompatible with each other. It is often useful to help the learner see that what has been taken to be simple, is, in fact, complex; or that what had seemed obvious is, in fact, dubious. Once the confusion is present, the learner can often be more open to deeper understandings of what was plain but simple.

3. Heighten the intensity of the motivation, perhaps by relating the material to the feelings, values, or thought-processes and experiences of the learner. Motivating forces which are intrinsically related to the learner's needs, the subject-matter, and the learning process are more educationally productive in the long run.

4. Increase the ability of the learner to take the initiative in the process of understanding. Beware of using the explanations of others as shortcut answers to the need to understand. Rather, use them as stimuli or points of comparison or as means

of helping define the problem more sharply or from a different angle.

5. The truth question and the variform ways of testing for truth always provide stimulus for further understanding. Often a teacher can provoke the truth test by devices as simple as asking the question, "Is that so? How do you know?" or by adopting the familiar devil's advocate stance on an issue.

6. One function of a teacher is to help provide awareness of alternative explanations. Sometimes the discovery that there are more than one viable explanations for the same event will stimulate inquiry for the more comprehensive understanding.

7. A teacher must be unwilling to allow students to stop with their preliminary understandings. The first "glow" of a new understanding can be a temptation to become a stopping-place for some students. The effective teacher will learn to recognize that achievement for what it is, value it, yet view it as either a temporary plateau or a potential starting-point from which to launch new inquiries.

8. When a learner seems to arrive at an understanding, the teacher can ask, "Now, you've got it, what can you do with it?" Not only will the attempt to use a new understanding provide a good test of the thoroughness and accuracy of the understanding. It may also deepen that understanding, extending the range of its implications and its connections with other understandings and areas of experience and study.

9. Fundamentally important, a teacher's own understanding must be always growing, changing, deepening, and broadening by being tested and refreshed by disciplined study, use, and enjoyment.

10. Perhaps even more important, certainly never to be forgot, is the joy of understanding itself. The "eureka experience," whether it comes suddenly or gradually, can be a deeply satisfying experience and a powerful educational motivation. The experience of having things "come together," of "seeing things whole," has its own intrinsic delight which ought not be minimized or forgot in the rush to implement.

11. Especially in the area of religion, a teacher needs to be constantly on the alert to help learners go beyond the facile mastery of the content. In religion, as in other areas, knowing

the facts (or even the stories, the doctrine, the ethics, the rituals, and even the organizational ins-and-outs) will not be an adequate substitute for understanding. In religion, especially, the teacher needs to find ways to help the learners encounter the content in dialectic with experience, with the past and the present; to see the content as constituted by something more complex and mysterious than words in the pages of a book. Yet the presence of a "mystery" cannot be taken as an excuse for backing off from the struggle to understand at full depth.

This need, grounded in the nature of religion and the understanding appropriate to it, would indicate that it is especially important in teaching religion to use methods which personally involve the learners, and hold promise of tapping not only the intellectual apprehension of religious phenomena but also the affective, conative, and spiritual dimensions. Unless the learner combines intellectual understanding with an understanding of these other dimensions of religion, there may be real question about attaining a full understanding of authentic religion.

However, this does not entail becoming a practicing believer in each religion one is attempting to understand. Just as one can understand another society or culture without subscribing personally to every part of that way of life, so one can have genuine understanding of a religion other than one's own without being committed to that religion.[12] Yet, as we have argued above, understanding that religion will entail the kind of empathetic attitude characterized by the term "being understanding" and the multi-dimensioned way of understanding appropriate to the nature of religion and religious life and community.

Such an expectation is not foreign to many approaches to education, as can be seen early in the works of John Dewey and George Albert Coe. They affirmed that the educational process itself can be seen as one of continuous self-transcendence, whose boundaries, if any, have yet to be seriously explored.

Notes

1. These observations can trace their roots directly to my serving as a teaching assistant with Randolph Crump Miller in a course in language analysis eventually distilled into his book, *The Language Gap and God.*

2. Jane R. Martin, *Explaining, Understanding and Teaching*, McGraw-Hill. 1970, pp. 143ff.
3. The framework for the description of understanding presented here was greatly informed by an excellent discussion by David Pole, "Understanding—A Physical Process," in the Proceedings of the Aristotelian Society, 1960, pp. 253–268.
4. Excellent discussions of this process can be found in Max Black, *Models and Metaphors* Cornell University Press, 1962, its religious application in Ian Ramsey, *Models and Mystery*, Oxford University Press, 1964, its educational application in Marc Belth, *Education as a Discipline*, Allyn & Bacon, 1965 and *New World of Education*, Allyn & Bacon, 1970, and its religious education application in my own "The Significance of Marc Belth for Religious Education," *Religious Education*, July-August, 1969.
5. A thorough and provocative description of this process can be found in James Loder, *Religious Pathology and Christian Faith*, The Westminster Press, 1966.
6. Bernard Lonergan, S. J., *Insight: A Study of Human Understanding*, Philosophical Library, 1970, especially pp. 82–83 and chapter IX.
7. R. K. Elliott presents an excellent list of criteria for one's having a fully developed understanding of a complex topic (which religion surely is) in "Education and Human Being," in *Philosophers Discuss Education*, edited by S. C. Brown, Macmillan, 1975; see especially pp. 47–48.
8. Suzanne Langer, *Philosophy in a New Key*, Harvard University Press, 1942. For a convenient summary of the brain research and its implications, see Robert Ornstein, *The Psychology of Consciousness*, Freeman, 1972.
9. Langer, *Philosophy in a New Key*, and Reid, "Feeling and Understanding," in *Aesthetic Concepts and Education*, Ralph Smith, University of Illinois Press, 1970, pp. 45–76.
10. Reid, ibid., p. 63.
11. John Wilson convincingly argues this position in his *Education in Religion and the Emotions*, Heinemann, 1970.
12. An excellent discussion of these concerns is found in Bryan Wilson, ed., *Rationality*, Blackwell, 1970, and especially in a discussion of that book by Gordon Reddiford, "Rationality and Understanding," *Philosophy*, Vol. 50, 1975, pp. 19–35.

CHAPTER 7

NAMING INTO PERSONHOOD: THE CHURCH'S EDUCATIONAL MINISTRY

David S. Steward and Margaret S. Steward

A. A MODEL

Naming is a creative act. This is especially true in the case of persons. Persons are called forth as they are named. It is our thesis that the process by which persons are named, first in the family and then beyond, reveals the structure of the church's educational ministry. We will express our thesis with the help of a "teacup model."[1]

The Work of Naming

To make a teacup, the potter begins with a lump of clay splattered lustily down in the middle of his wheel. In a few swift turns it is centered, and suddenly it ceases to be inert. It becomes a pliant, surging force responsive to the pressure and tone of the potter's hand. It is no longer dissectable. It may not be separated either from itself or from the potter's wheel. It becomes alive to the touch and tension of the artist and moves up and out fluidly—whole to whole. During each instant of throwing it is all, and that all is constantly in flux. It is finished, not when enough is added, but when the hand is removed to leave the shape most pleasing to the artist's eye and skill.

To think of potting is to think as an artist. Yet there are similarities between art-thought and science-thought which we want to note and celebrate. In her recent book on the family, *The Intimate Environment*,[2] Arlene Skolnick insists that *families* can be a unit in terms of which to think about the dynamics and meaning of life. Families are complex wholes. It is somewhat strange to think of one whole, a family, made up of many wholes, family members, but that's how it *works*. And the "how it works" dimension is important. If we insist on analytic perfection, then a family can only be a mother plus a father plus some assortment of children. But in our *experience* families aren't formulas. They're events. *Working* is what families are about. And in affirming this we invite families to join other enigmas, like schools and villages and churches, which are best understood in their *work*.

What can we say about the *work* in terms of which we come to understand a family? Not much is required. It's rather like the potter's clay. For the potter the clay came, became, came into being as it was splattered, turned, centered, shaped. Families come, become, come into being—*are*—as they move, interact, relate, communicate. In the loving, working hands of the potter a miracle happens. Without changing, a lump becomes a cup. With similar loving work, families happen. Virginia Satir names the process *peoplemaking*.[3] And that's just what it is. Families are peoplemakers, and the work which makes them so is the planful, touchful, motionful, respectful work which the potter exhibits in his art. We call that work *naming*.

Books have been written about how people become. The perspective we are urging is that of a systems theory which works organically and, in Jerome Bruner's phrase, "beyond the information given."[4] The focal point of our teacup model is the patterned activity of people, where the personhood is the communion effected by work and by the meaning symbolized in that work *which is beyond the behaviors themselves*. Some call it feeling; some call it love. It is what families do and are. And the result is a new person. Identity is the fruit of one family and the seed of the next. All the personhood I can claim comes from the work-gift I know as family. That gift empowers me to work-give, and thereby to come to be partner in family crafting. This is how naming *works*.

It is in the boundaries that shape is given. How can we look at the edges by which a family names? The potter presses and squeezes until the proper edges emerge. This is our experience

in family-craft as well. The naming edges we shall explore are
the edges of history and society.

The Cup of History

Every family is a blend. If you've ever diagrammed your
family tree, even for a couple of generations, you know the
incredibly complex content which fills the teacup of generations. Ivan Boszormenyi-Nagy and his colleague Geraldine
Spark note the inevitability of that content. They say, "We can
terminate any relationship except the one based on parenting;
in reality, we cannot select our parents or children."[5]

Despite this arbitrariness, there are what Nagy and Spark call
"invisible loyalties" which bind us to our ancestors. What binds
families is partly the biological endowment which runs through
them. In our own family we have four generations of people
who are good mathematicians, but who write and spell poorly,
who invert phone numbers and who have to work hard to
orient a map. This provides a common experience across the
generations which gives our family a distinctive flavor.

More subtle, but perhaps even more powerful, are the an-
cestral myths and stories which are the available library we use
in the interpretation of family events. Given a large enough
family tree, there will be a memory to match nearly every new
milestone of growing up. So it is that baby Jane has Aunt Sue's
nose; or young Peter gets red in the face when he's angry, just
like Uncle George. The origin of a family myth is historical.
However, it may be rooted in as few as a single family experience. The extension of the myth to a new person is a product as
much of the mindset and expectations of the observer, as it is of
an accurate comparison of color of skin or tone of voice. And
that's what gives family myth its power. Myth incorporates easily whomever we choose to incorporate. *Any* child may belong to
us, because our imaginations may be stretched with infinite
variability. The act which includes the child is up to us.

Oral tradition gathers up and focuses family memories on an
individual. This process announces to the family and to the
world at large the right of the child to belong to this particular
group. The inclusion of the child in the family myth-system by
stretching the stories to include him is a way of claiming the

child—baptizing, some would say. Part of what the teacup of generations contains is a story or myth-system which permits bridging within families and across times so that a new member may belong, and through belonging learn to become part of this particular family.

The Saucer of Society

Most cups "run over"—or at least spill, from time to time. Families and family-trees are neither isolated nor isolatable in a world busy with social institutions and arrangements. Families, like teacups, need saucers—arenas to catch the spill, and to provide the awareness that there is a context for family affairs.

Theodore Lidz says that persons have two endowments. They are born with a biological endowment, and they are born into a cultural endowment.[6] The family has a context. It is surrounded by a culture with which it interpenetrates. Although saucers and teacups are often interchangeable—a witness to the adaptability of persons in society—the less satisfactory the fit, the more risk there is that the teacup, when carried, will wobble, fall, and break. This is the experience which many native Americans fear. Particularly in the severe environment of the Arctic North Slope, technology has a social impact. The modified environment becomes a new saucer, and the traditional cup, carefully fashioned to fit another setting, comes to be more and more precariously balanced. Eskimo and Indian ways are at risk—some would say with a sickness unto death.

Heinz Hartmann has introduced a conceptual scheme to help us think about this interface of the teacup and saucer. He spoke of the match, at birth, between the infant and "an average expectable environment."[7] The world is prepared and able to receive us—which means that, even at birth, we fit, and thereby belong. This is a way of expressing the wholeness and integrity which we experience in our world.

Erik Erikson has extended Hartmann's match between infant and world to cover the entire life-cycle. His eight stages of human development symbolize the presence of psycho-social crises and resolutions from birth to death.[8] Stated in a more radical form, each moment of living reveals an interaction, a transaction, a match between the person and the world. Whether or not the cup wobbles in the saucer, the saucer is *there*, containing the fragile structure of the cup.

The interface between family and society is explicitly behavioral. Where family myth, storytelling and memory characterize the content of the cup, patterns of behavior involving the larger society surface with the saucer.

Naming is a complex social act. It assumes a social structure in which relationship is the fundamental term. It requires a community of interpretation which stretches backwards in time, thereby providing myths and stories which serve to identify and claim the new person. It occurs in the midst of patterns of interaction through which the larger society interfaces with the family and which fit the individual and family into larger group membership. The equation which our model reveals is that "story plus act are needed for naming."

B. EDUCATIONAL MINISTRY

It is our proposal that education involves naming. Therefore, it demands a community intentionally living a tradition. When the community is the church, and when the intentionality refers to the Judeo-Christian tradition, we have what we call "educational ministry." We want to identify three points of reference to which we must return in educational ministry, if we want to name into Christian personhood.

Naming by the Church

First, we want to speak of worship. Paul Tillich calls the intersection of sacred time and human experience a point of power.[9] In the experience of the Christian, this is worship. It is a meeting—as Quakers call it—in which story and action merge. In worship we remember, and in worship we act—in symbolic ways which draw the entire scope of tradition and living into a focused moment of power. In the event of worship, everything changes. We are born anew, and new names become appropriate.

Baptism is the prototypical form of the worship we are describing. In baptism a child (and in some communions, an adult) is brought forth in sacred time and *named*. As is the case with the family, the giving of the name is accomplished by the community, and the community assumes, in that gift, a parenting responsibility. The name-giving does not, magically, *make* the child Christian. It represents the intention of the community to impute Christian status to the child—to look on the child as Christian, and therefore, with God's help, to act toward the child in ways which will permit him to view himself as a child of God and member of the Christian family.

We would argue that this is precisely the function of every meeting for worship. By remembering what God has done for us and by symbolizing our living responses to God's gift, we find ourselves in a moment of power which turns us around, calling us to be whom God has named us, in the details of living. Where a congregation worships, people are called to be, and empowered to become. This first, recurring naming by the church is at the heart of educational ministry.

Naming by the Family

Second, we want to speak of "the everyday." This point of reference for educational ministry has a dialectical relationship to the first. The life of community is more than occasional peak experiences. It is in the elusive space we now call "the everyday" that the structure of our living unfolds. Horace Bushnell speaks of the "charactered Christian" who expresses the face of Jesus Christ in the habit forms of daily living.[10] Such action he calls "religion of the hearth" and, for him, it is the basic human contribution to Christian nurture.

This second Christian naming is focused during the preschool years within the intimacy of the family. Through the expectations engendered by family myths and through patterns of interaction between child and family, the family's orientation—its ethnicity—is taught. Christians are an ethnic group too. We have a specific tradition and call. We are required to increase the love of God and neighbor.

The "religion of the hearth" makes operational our tradition and call. Educational ministry rests on the everydayness of our witness. The details of our living must be distinctive if our children are to know us as Christians, and through this "looking-glass" find themselves and their worth reflected in our active love toward them.

Naming by the World

Finally, we want to speak of "going forth." This third point of reference for educational ministry forces us beyond the church family toward its interface with the world. It is one thing to know ourselves within the womb of those who love us. It is another thing to be compared, critically, with persons and agencies beyond ourselves. Educational ministry must not stop with the warm inclusiveness of a community separated from the rest of life. Knowing ourselves as Christians is to know that we must venture. Abraham "went forth." Jesus commanded: "Go into all the world." The sanctuary is a place for gathering strength; it is not a terminal point.

Until Christians "go forth" to the intersection with a world full of persons and agencies—to be compared and criticized by them—the third Christian naming will not happen. The church, made up as it is of people, must be named by the world, or it will shrivel in its own introverted piety, and die. And that means that you and I will die, as Christians, for it is we who are the church incarnate. This is a danger these days as churches face a world that *will* compare them and question their competence to contribute to the community's survival. The church is challenged these days to tell its story to the world by what it does. The church cannot rest on a caricatured nickname; it must not be ignored into namelessness. The self-esteem gained in the power of worship expressed through the religion of the hearth can, with God's help, carry us with confidence and competence apparent to all into a struggling, pluralistic world. The naming of the church by the community is the major test of our times. It is the challenge which most presses now on educational ministry.

The church, through its educational ministry, can name into Christian personhood when it roots itself in the moment of meeting we experience in worship; when it routinizes its lifestyle in everyday responses of love; and when it ventures forth into the world to be compared and named itself, according to its competence.

Notes

1. A model always shapes experience in limited and arbitrary ways. The "teacup model" focuses on the social-historical roots of personhood. It is important to remember that there is organizing, integrative power in each person which qualifies all social roots. A psycho-historical model will accompany "the teacup" in a comprehensive treatment of naming into personhood.
2. Arlene Skolnick, *The Intimate Environment*, Little, Brown and Co., 1973.
3. Virginia Satir, *Peoplemaking*, Science and Behavior Books, 1972.
4. Jerome S. Bruner, *Beyond the Information Given*, ed. Jeremy M. Anglin, W. W. Norton and Co., 1973
5. Ivan Boszormenyi-Nagy and Geraldine M. Spark, *Invisible Loyalties*, Harper & Row, 1973.
6. Theodore Lidz, *The Family and Human Adaptation*, International Universities Press, 1962.
7. Heinz Hartmann, *Ego Psychology and the Problem of Adaptation*, International Universities Press, 1958.
8. Erik H. Erikson, *Childhood and Society*, W. W. Norton and Co., 1950.
9. Paul Tillich, *The Protestant Era*, University of Chicago Press, 1948.
10. Horace Bushnell, *Christian Nurture*, Yale University Press, new ed., 1947.

CHAPTER 8

DIALOGUE WITH WHITEHEAD'S PROCESS GOD

Ewert H. Cousins

Whitehead's doctrine of God has stimulated an ongoing dialogue which has explored the relation between the process God and the traditional God of Christian faith. On the one hand, this dialogue has been critical of Whitehead, claiming that his doctrine of God is incompatible with Christian belief. On the other hand, his doctrine has been singled out as the most appropriate metaphysical articulation of the God of biblical revelation and Christian faith.[1]

There has been a third strand in this dialogue, in which Whitehead's God has evoked a clarification of the Christian doctrine of God and has stimulated constructive Christian theology. It is not surprising that in many instances this strand of the dialogue has focused on the trinity, for the doctrine of the trinity has been the unique and quintessential expression of Christian belief in God. Furthermore, Whitehead's doctrine of God gives forceful articulation to dynamism and relatedness—two aspects of the divinity which have been expressed traditionally through the Christian doctrine of the trinity.

The elements of this dialogue with the trinity are provided by Whitehead's distinction between the primordial and consequent nature of God and by his notion of creativity. God's transcendence is rooted in his primordial nature, in which "he is the unlimited conceptual realization of the absolute wealth of potentiality."[2] As primordial, he is deficient in actuality; however, the realization of possibilities within the temporal process leads to the enrichment of God in his consequent nature. According to Whitehead, God in his consequent nature "shares with every new creation its actual world; and the concrescent creature is objectified in God as a novel element in God's objectification of that actual world."[3] In this way God is enriched by the temporal process. This polarity which Whitehead sees between the primordial and consequent natures of God has some resonance with the divine polarities expressed in the doctrine of the trinity. If one adds to Whitehead's dipolar notion of God his concept of creativity, then the resonance with the trinity is even more discernible, since creativity adds a third principle. Whitehead, however, does not speak of creativity as a distinct pole in God, but assigns it to the category of the ultimate, with both God and the world sharing in creativity. In so doing, he may seem to subordinate God to creativity. These Whiteheadian elements and their complex relationship, then, set the stage for a fruitful dialogue with the doctrine of the trinity.

In one of the earliest studies of Whitehead's philosophy, Dorothy Emmet established a dialogue with the trinity by taking her point of departure from Whitehead's notion of creativity.[4] She observed that in Whitehead creativity seems to be prior to God. "Is creativity prior to God?" Emmet asks. Or in reality are creativity and the primordial nature of God "complementary sides of the same thing?"[5] She claims that this is similar to the problem, investigated by the Greek fathers, of the relation of the first and second persons of the trinity—a problem which gave rise to the Arian controversy. In a most insightful move, Emmet correlates Whitehead's creativity to the Father in the trinity and the primodial nature of God to the Son: "We may look on creativity as analogous to the Creative Power of the Father, and the Primordial Nature of God as analogous to the Logos—the order of a 'Wisdom' in virtue of which effective creation is possible."[6] She goes on to correlate the Holy Spirit with Whitehead's consequent nature of God, "as the measure of creative order achieved in the world."[7] Emmet's methodology is clearly that of dialogue; she is not trying to identify Whitehead's doctrine of God with the trinity, but to point out "analogies" and to indicate how the two are dealing with common problems.

In an article entitled "Process Trinitarianism," Lewis Ford continues the dialogue between Whitehead's process God and the Christian trinity.[8] Like Emmet, Ford correlates the second person or Logos with the primordial nature. He states that the Logos preeminently symbolizes and exemplifies the primordial nature, "for Logos is structure and order, and the primordial nature is the complete, timeless ordering of all formal structures."[9] Ford goes on to discuss the Father from a Whiteheadian perspective. "Insofar as the Word symbolizes the whole of the primordial nature, the symbol Father is freed to point to the ultimate transcendent source of the manifest structure."[10] For Whitehead, according to Ford, this ultimate transcendent source is "the primordial envisagement, that nontemporal act of divine self-creation which issues forth as the complete ordering of all eternal objects which is the primordial nature."[11] This position seems very close to that of Emmet and, in fact, may be substantially identical with it. Like Emmet, Ford goes on to discuss the Spirit in terms of the consequent nature; but he warns that "any simple identification of the Spirit with the consequent nature would only produce confusion."[12]

In a number of articles I have attempted to join this dialogue, moving in a direction similar to that of Emmet and Ford.[13] These articles have drawn into the dialogue Bonaventure, the thirteenth century philosopher-theologian, whose thought is profoundly trinitarian and who developed a doctrine of God as dynamic and intimately related to the world. Deriving elements both from the Greek fathers and from Augustine, Bonaventure elaborated a doctrine of the Father as primordial creative source and of the Logos as the locus of the 'eternal reasons' or the divine ideas which are the grounding within God of all intelligible forms in creation. For Bonaventure the Father is the *fontalis plenitudo,* the fountain-fullness who expresses himself in his word or Logos; and in so expressing himself, he simultaneously expresses the possibilities of all that he can create. In Bonaventure, then, I find a similarity with the trinitarian model that emerges out of the correlations made by Emmet and Ford with Whitehead's process God.

It is important, however, to make a certain precision at this point. For Bonaventure, the creativity of the Father in generating the Son—as well as the Son himself and the Spirit—are eminently real and actual prior to the actualization of possibilities in the temporal process. In this Bonaventure's God sharply differs from the primordial nature which is described by Whitehead as being deficient in actuality.[14] Being eternally actual in an eminent way, the Father, Son, and Spirit in their divine dynamism are the ground of all dynamism within the temporal process. The preeminent actuality of God in himself may constitute the point of greatest divergence of the classical doctrine of God from Whitehead's position. However, it must be noted that in Bonaventure's tradition—as is clear from the correlations of Emmet and Ford—the trinity is dynamic and related; hence classical theism, at least in its trinitarian form, may not be so far removed from the Whiteheadian process God as some interpreters have judged.

In this present study, I would like to extend my own dialogue with Whitehead's process God one step further. Following in the direction of Emmet and Ford and that of my previous articles on Bonaventure, I will focus on the Father. But I will go beyond the Father as creative source of the Son, beyond the act of primordial envisagement and the Father's fountain-fullness. I will move to another pole of the divinity—from the Father as creative to the Father as silence. In so doing, I will propose a dipolar model of God, inspired by Whitehead's dipolar doctrine of God, but at the same time quite different. I will make the following claim: God is indeed dipolar, but not merely in relation to the world, so that we can discern a primordial and a consequent nature. God is also dipolar in himself. One can detect a dipolarity within the trinity itself, as is suggested by Emmet's analysis of creativity and the primordial nature. In this perspective, one could see the Father and Son as dipolar, with the Spirit as the union of the two poles of the divinity. I acknowledge this dipolarity within the trinity, but propose here another and deeper dipolarity. Basically it consists in the following. Within himself God has a nonmanifesting pole and a manifesting pole. This nonmanifesting pole is the divine silence out of which speech springs; it is the divine darkness out of which light flows; it is the abyss of the divinity out of which the divine self-manifestation emerges. The trinity in its total formality—of creativity, expression and union, or Father, Son, and Spirit—constitutes the manifesting pole of the divinity.

Although the nonmanifesting pole has a certain priority of origin, I maintain that both of these poles are consubstantially divine. There is no question here of subordinationism. I do not wish to fall into a neo-Arianism and subordinate the trinity to the transcendent deity, placing the manifesting pole of God ontologically on the side of creation. I do not wish to make the nonmanifesting pole of God a "godhead above God" or a "super-essential godhead" which alone can be called truly God in contrast with the subordinate pole of the manifesting divinity. On the contrary, I maintain as essential to my position that these two poles—the nonmanifesting and the manifesting—are equally divine. This is precisely what leads me to speak of this as a dipolar doctrine, meaning by the term a consubstantial dipolarity.

In order to affirm this consubstantial dipolarity more precisely, it would be helpful to speak of a certain dipolarity of the Father. From this perspective, the nonmanifesting pole of the divinity could be given the name of the Father, but with the understanding that this is the Father as silence, darkness, or abyss. The name Father would also refer to the other pole and would include the meaning of creativity whereby the Son is generated and the Spirit spirated. This twofold understanding of the name Father would express the dipolarity of the divinity in such a way that the consubstantiality of the two poles would be affirmed. It must be noted that the manifesting pole of the divinity in its fullness includes the total trinity, the Father, Son, and Spirit, since the Father as actualized creativity expresses himself in his Son and is united to the Son in the Spirit.

It may seem that my journey into the silence of the Father has taken us far from Whitehead's God. In a certain sense that is true, for Whitehead's God is oriented to the world and even changed by the temporal process. The Whiteheadian approach is concerned with cosmology and natural theology; whereas the trinity is associated with revelation, and the silence of the Father is the realm of mystical intuition rather than intellectual speculation. It is true that I have taken the dialogue with Whitehead's process God one step beyond the stage articulated by Emmet and Ford. I believe that such a move is important not only for exploring alternate models of God, but also for extending the dialogue on God into the Christian mystical tradition and into the contemporary encounter with world religions.

Certain Christian mystics have presented a doctrine of God which has seemed to some interpreters to threaten Christian orthodoxy. For in the final stages of their mystical ascent, they reach like Meister Eckhardt the "godhead above God," or like the Pseudo-Dionysius the "super-essential godhead." In these cases they seem to leave the trinity behind on a subordinate level of reality and thus fall into a form of Arianism. I claim that this problem is avoided by my model of dipolar consubstantiality on the level of the nonmanifesting and manifesting poles of the divinity. At the same time contact is made with a most important strand of the Christian mystical tradition.

Contact with this Christian mystical current is especially important at the present time when the great religious traditions of the world are encountering one another in an open and creative climate. The dialogue between Christianity and world religions can proceed from a number of points of view, but one of the most significant of these is undoubtedly that of the doctrine of God or ultimate reality. In this respect, on the Christian side pioneer work has been done by Raimundo Panikkar in his work *The Trinity and the Religious Experience of Man.*[15] Taking his point of departure from the Christian doctrine of the trinity, Panikkar establishes contact with the silence of Buddhism, but relating it to the silence of the Father. He correlates the nondifferentiated unity of the advaitan Hindu tradition with the unity of the Spirit. Judaism, Christianity and Islam are seen as religions of revelation, of the word or Logos. Panikkar's work in this direction opens another avenue of approach which could complement the work being done by John Cobb to establish a dialogue between Whiteheadian thought and Buddhism.[16] The silence of the Father is without doubt a point of convergence of many theological, mystical, and speculative currents and merits investigation from many points of view.

This present study has merely attempted to sketch the direction that has been taken and might be pursued by one strand of the dialogue with Whitehead's process God. I acknowledge, of course, the need for a technical exploration of issues which is beyond the scope of this brief chapter. In sketching this dialogue, I have moved from the primordial nature of Whitehead's God, to the Christian trinity, to the Christian mystical tradition, and then to the dialogue of world religions. There is another possible move and one which could be at least equally fruitful: namely a move in the direction of the consequent nature and towards the interrelation of God and the world. It may be that Whitehead's notion of the interaction of God and the world is his most seminal contribution to a dialogue on God. It is this aspect of God that Randolph Crump Miller has explored; e.g., in his article "Empiricism and Process Theology: God is What God Does."[17] In "the creative advance into novelty,"[18] both God and the world are mutually involved in creativity. Echoing the previous phase of the dialogue, we could say that the silence of the Father issues in many levels of expression. On the level of temporal process, the speech is a joint articulation between God and the world. The world has something of its own to say, something of importance which contributes to the fullness of reality. But this is another phrase of the dialogue which we can only point to here and hope to explore in a similar vein at some future time.

Notes

1. Cf. the reactions to Whitehead's doctrine of God surveyed by Gene Reeves and Delwin Brown, "The Development of Process Theology," in *Process Philosophy and Christian Thought*, ed. Delwin Brown, Ralph E. James, Jr., and Gene Reeves, Bobbs-Merrill, 1971, pp. 21-64.
2. Alfred North Whitehead, *Process and Reality*, Macmillan, 1929, p. 521.
3. Ibid., p. 523.
4. Dorothy Emmet, *Whitehead's Philosophy of Organism*, Macmillan, 1932, pp. 252-258.
5. Ibid., p. 252.
6. Ibid., p. 253.
7. Ibid., p. 255.
8. Lewis S. Ford, "Process Trinitarianism," *Journal of the American Academy of Religion*, 43 (1975), 199-213.
9. Ibid., p. 205.
10. Ibid., p. 206.
11. Loc. cit.
12. Loc. cit.
13. Ewart H. Cousins, "Truth in St. Bonaventure," *Proceedings of the American Catholic Philosophical Association*, 43 (1969), 204-210; "Bonaventure

and Process Thought," *Listening,* 9 (1974), 54–71; "God as Dynamic in Bonaventure and Contemporary Thought," *Proceedings of the American Catholic Philosophical Association,* 48 (1974), 136–148; "Bonaventure and Contemporary Thought," *The Cord,* 25 (1975), 68–78; "La temporalié de Dieu dans la thólogie du devenir (Process Theology)," in *Temporalité et aliénation,* ed. Enrico Castelli, Aubier, 1975, pp. 139–159.

14. Cf. Cousins, "La temporalité de Dieu dans la théologie du devenir (Process Theology)," 152–159.

15. Raimundo Panikkar, *The Trinity and the Religious Experience of Man,* Orbis Books, 1973; cf. Ewert H. Cousins, "The Trinity and World Religions," *Journal of Ecumenical Studies,* 7 (1970), 476–498.

16. John B. Cobb, Jr., *Christ in a Pluralistic Age,* The Westminster Press, 1975, pp. 203–220; with Ryusei Takeda, "'Mosa-Dharma' and Prehension: Nigarjuna and Whitehead Compared," *Process Studies,* 4 (1974), 26–36.

17. Randolph Crump Miller, "Empiricism and Process Theology: God is What God Does," *The Christian Century,* 93 (1976), 284–287.

18. Whitehead, op. cit., pp. 196, 340, 529.

CHAPTER 9

BEING AND NONBEING IN PRE-SOCRATIC PHILOSOPHY

Theodore A. McConnell

Being is one of the elementary, fundamental concepts that must be perennially examined and depicted in the history of philosophy. Much of the recent rhetoric about nonbeing, especially among the existentialist philosophers, reminds us again of this elementary starting-point for philosophic systems. Turning to ancient philosophy is likely to provide a clarified understanding of the importance of being and of its implications for later thought, including that of recent process philosophies. This chapter presents a category list or index of the concept in pre-Socratic philosophy, together with brief commentaries, and a final summary and analysis. In turning to these earliest of philosophers, I shall note some rudimentary ideas of process, just as the idea of process proves to be an important element in resolving the basic dilemmas of being and nonbeing.

HERACLITUS: BEING AS CHANGE

Heraclitus' teaching is probably the first instance in which being was considered as such in ancient philosophy. More primitive considerations are to be found in the reports of Thales' ideas and in those of Anaximander and Anaximenes, but these concern the original state out of which the world developed (the *arche* as water for Thales and air for Anaximenes). It is with Heraclitus, however, that the idea of being appears and is explicitly developed.

Nothing remains without change. Everything is in a continuum. The fact of change is the only changeless. Stability seems to appear, but such is illusion. The infinite flux constitutes reality.

Heraclitus' relativism is striking although he was more subdued in his arguments than those of his pupil Cratylus. Nevertheless, for Heraclitus it remains doubtful if one can acquire any nonillusory knowledge. The only infinite is change, which is synonymous with being. Humankind cannot know anything and cannot have any basis for taking those actions that appear to maintain existence.

CRATYLUS: BEING AS ULTIMATE AND EXTREME CHANGE

The flux and flow is so all-embracing that one cannot ever step into a river even once. For not only is the river continually changing, but so is the individual.

Here we have Heraclitus' concept taken to its ultimate and final conclusion. The river is never the same; nothing is the same; indeed, we cannot "fix" or "hold" anything for a solitary moment in order to experience or understand it. Even enunciation of the principle is impossible, for it falls under the flux and flow of the universe. Being is infinite change and there is nothing further to be said; one can simply experience its ever-changing reality.

PARMENIDES: BEING AS INFINITE

That nonbeing is and that it necessarily is, I call a wholly incredible course, since thou canst not recognize nonbeing (for this is impossible) nor couldst thou speak of it, for thought and being are the same thing.

Being is without beginning and indestructible; it is universal, existing alone, immovable and without end; nor ever was it nor will it be, since it now is, all together, one and continuous. For what generating of it wilt thou seek? From what did it grow, and how? I will not permit thee to say or to think that it came from nonbeing; for it is impossible to think or say that nonbeing is. What thing would then have stirred it into activity that it should arise from nonbeing later than earlier? But since there is a final limit, it is perfected on every side, like the mass of a rounded sphere, equally distant from the center at every point.

Parmenides is perhaps the first philosopher to have developed such a definite and precise conviction regarding the impossibility of nonbeing. The part of his eighth *Fragment* quoted exposes the most loosely constructed part of his definition of being. In postulating a limit to being in an analogical way as a sphere of absolute perfection, Parmenides never specifically defined the nature of the limit. In this regard the appropriate question is, if there is an ultimate limitation to being, what is its nature? And does it derive from being itself? If the limitation does not derive from being, is it the opposite of being (certainly not possible for Parmenides); is it otherness of being (then it derives from being); or is it simply the boundary of being?

It is possible that Parmenides' principle of limitation of being involves including the finite within being's infinite nature, for being certainly is conceived as infinite. Parmenides' idea of being is significant because it demonstrates such an explicit and absolute attempt to establish the impossibility of nonbeing. In so doing, its implications cannot be evaded. His perspective is one of the basic positions and points of reference in ancient philosophy and has probably not been improved upon much since his original formulation. Melissus and Empedocles restated the position, working essentially from negation, but the shock effect and impressive impact of Parmenides' precision remains in arguing so explicitly that once one has said that something is, one is debarred from saying that it was or will be.

ANAXAGORAS: BEING AS GROUNDED IN QUANTATIVE PARADOX

For neither is there a least of what is small, but there is always a less. For being is not nonbeing. But there is always a greater than what is great. And it is equal to the small in number; but with reference to itself each thing is both small and great.

For nothing comes into being nor yet does anything perish, but there is mixture and separation of things that are.

Anaxagoras defined being as infinite and a type of ground

from which "mixture" and "separation" flow, but in which there is no new generation and no new coming into being. The quantative idea of being rests in a paradoxical situation in which there is the potential of the limitless or unlimited in contrast to the limited (the "least of what is small" and the "greater than what is great"). It is a strange paradox and yet it should not be dismissed without some consideration.

Finiteness is of basic significance in understanding Anaxagoras' idea of being. This reminds us that a basic characteristic of finiteness is limitation, which allows for its measurement in contrast to the immeasurability of the infinite. In comparison with those who see being as simply infinite, Anaxagoras' idea may be more illuminating in this regard for he chose to see being as analogous to a quantative paradox: Being is the basis of existence and yet not itself existent in any temporal-spatial way. Being is related to the finite world and yet is not finite in itself or part of a finite world. Here is a polar idea of being which, if taken to its conclusion, allows each existing entity to open up new potentialities in its flowing process of existence. This nascent "process" idea of being and becoming in which being exists within the finite but is unlimited, allows for infinite potentiality within existence. Being is an infinite functioning in relation to the finite, and there is no nonbeing.

DEMOCRITUS: NONBEING AS THE VOID

There are only atoms and the void. This is all of reality.
Objects of the senses are not real, only atoms and the void are real.
The vortex is the necessary cause of all things. No thing can come into being from nothing and no thing can pass away into nothing.
Causation is grounded in necessity and this stems from the void.

For Democritus, atoms were being, the vortex was the locus of mixing and separation, and the "void" was distinct and different from the atoms and the vortex. The void is not made up of particles, and mixing or separation are not connected with it. Change and being are temporal, concrete, and limited entities, whereas the vortex is quite different, although it may have relationship to change and being. The void is beyondness, for Democritus, and in essence he argued that it is fundamental to being and change. So nonbeing or the void assumes priority to and necessity for being and change.

GORGIAS: BEING AND NONBEING AS NOTHING—EXTREME RELATIVISM

> For if Non-Being does exist it will both be and not be at the same time. In so far as it is considered as not being it will not be, and in so far as it is considered as Not-Being it will be.

In Gorgias "to be" or "exist" is used in a conventional manner (i.e., existing as objective, tangible, of specific location) that creates insuperable difficulties. To speak in concrete terms and categories about a universal such as being leads to unnecessary confusion and false conclusions. For example, the contradiction that Gorgias thought he had identified in being, is actually due to his attempts to think about being in concrete, specific categories.

Ultimately, Gorgias' position was contradictory for if, as he argued, nothing can be known and being cannot be, this is an affirmation of sorts. Gorgias' extreme relativism, if consistent, could assert nothing, including any affirmation of itself, yet he continued to write and speak. The result is less than convincing and leaves little promise of further explication and knowledge.

NASCENT IDEAS OF BEING AND BECOMING

The problem of nonbeing ultimately resides in two related matters. First, can nonbeing have meaning and if so, what is its meaning? And second, can nonbeing as a term and category denote an actual, concrete, independent force or entity apart from being? In other words, can there exist apart from being a force or entity that either potentially or actually threatens being?

With regard to the first question, can nonbeing have meaning, it is important to distinguish types of meaning. Two fundamental types or categories of meaning are *intensional* meaning, in which the term or name refers to no concrete, actual or existential object (the name of a class which has no objects or is null; a mental class) and *extensional* meaning, in which the name or term is meaningful in reference or relation to some concrete, existential object. (Among the latter there are also generalized meanings in which a definition or meaning is derived by *intensional* means from specific properties and concrete objects.)

At that moment when a name or term comes to indicate or refer to a specific object or class of objects, it denotes an instance of being. Therefore the term nonbeing can have no *extensional* meaning. To place nonbeing in existence (of something) is an error that involves making a nonconcrete name (with no referent) the referent to something. It would seem that when one speaks of the "threat of nonbeing to existence," or of the actuality of nonbeing "beyond" the limitation of being, as has been done in some recent philosophy and theology, then a misplaced judgment has occurred. The *intensional* and *extensional* have been mixed and the result at best is confusion. *Intensionally* speaking, nonbeing may have meaning apart from all *extensional* thought, but such meaning is in the nature of a distinction with respect to the diverse nature of being and has no concrete, existential reference.

Nonbeing has often been defined as the negation of being. In this respect the fundamental issue that must be considered is, can there occur absolute or universal negation of being? The contention "there can be a total negation of being"—without remainder—is itself assertive of being. For example, the premises "nonbeing is," "nonbeing exists," or "nonbeing can be," are self-contradictory. This kind of self-contradictory premise is meaningless and has no validity. Any negation of being is accomplished as a negation of a specific instance of being (that is, an *extensional* instance of being). Nevertheless, there can be no negation of universal being or being as such. This assertion is similar to that of Alfred North Whitehead's, who regarded negation as meaningful only in relation to the concrete or actual.[1] Whitehead's stance is applicable to the negation of universal being in that it becomes *extensionally* meaningless to discuss negation of being as such.

If, as I have suggested, nonbeing is an *extensionally* meaningless or false term, what characterizes that force within the nature of being which so many philosophers have named nonbeing? Plato spoke of the "otherness of being," while Aristotle

believed there was an aspect or state of being which he described as ignorance or privation of knowledge. Perhaps this
"otherness" state should be described as that aspect of being
which encompasses the impossible or meaningless in relation to
the possible and occasions of past actuality. It is the *intensional*
idea of the impossible which can never receive actualization. As
such it is *extensionally* meaningless. This aspect of being, the
"otherness" that encompasses the impossible, can be further
described in terms of Whitehead's negative prehension. In *Process and Reality*, Whitehead wrote: "A negative prehension is the
definite exclusion of that item from positive contribution to the
subject's own real internal constitution. This doctrine involves
the position that a negative prehension expresses a bond."[2] The
"otherness" of being may, like negative prehension, be thought
of as a bond; it does not make a conclusive contribution to the
internal structure of being and yet it is an aspect of being. The
relationship is more one of limitation and exclusion than anything else.

In thinking about being, it is imperative to avoid making
being as such the ultimate and universal category for it involves
limitation in terms of nonbeing. Being is not the ultimate category and yet there can be no universal negation of being. And
so one must address the question of being's status and nature.
The five fundamental categories of pre-Socratic philosophy
present some of the basic options for understanding being—as
change, the infinite, a quantative paradox, the void, and nothing. The logical liabilities and flaws in these have been briefly
examined and their basic differences are evident. A similar
consideration of the rest of ancient philosophy and of medieval
philosophy is necessary for a more adequate understanding of
this subject. Nevertheless, sufficient material has been considered to establish the point that many later and contemporary
problems in thinking about being and nonbeing can readily be
perceived when attention is given to ancient philosophy. In
Parmenides one finds a definite and firm idea of being and
an argument against the possibility of nonbeing and in Anaxagoras a nascent process idea of being and becoming. It is
this process idea of relationship between being and becoming
that was to develop, albeit somewhat erratically, in the history

of philosophy and that illuminates and clarifies the nature of being. That is another chapter that needs to be written in due course.

Notes

1. Alfred North Whitehead, *Process and Reality*, The Humanities Press edition, 1957, p. 372.
2. Ibid., p. 66.

PART III

RELATIONSHIPS, HUMAN AND DIVINE: ASPECTS OF PROCESS THEOLOGY

CHAPTER 10

SEXISM AND GOD-TALK: TWO MODELS OF RELATIONSHIP

Rosemary Radford Ruether

The God-human relationship acts as a primary model for relationship in general; both as a model of relationship to the self and relationship to others. This means that the God-human relationship can be a prophetic means of elevating and transforming human relationships. But it also means, unfortunately, that human societies have projected their own models of oppressive social and psychic relationships upon the God-human picture and used this projected image to sanction such oppressive relationships in society and in the self. In this essay I wish to examine to contrasting models of relationship in the Christian tradition.

The dominant model for God-human relationship has been a hierarchical one. God as the "source of our being" has been construed that God is like a dominating, all-powerful king who reduces his "subjects" to a state of total dependency and obedience. Autonomy and self-direction in the self are construed as an insurrection against one's divine sovereign. God relates to his creation an omnipotent Subject manipulating a passive object that is totally directed by the divine Will. These models of divine-human relationship, in turn, sanction similar relations of mastery and sovereignty in human relations: (1) in the relation of the ego to the body and the physical creation; (2) in the relationship of kings and lords to subjects and lower classes, and (3) the relation of males to females. "Wives be subject to your husbands as the church is subject to Christ, for the husband is the head of the wife as Christ is the head of the church, his body"—this kind of language makes a divine-human relationship of head over body, mastery and subjugation the analogy for male-female relationships in marriage.

The divine-human model of domination and subjugation tends to translate itself into mutually exclusive dualisms of nature and grace, divine will and human will. Translated into human terms, God is pictured as a peculiarly neurotic, authoritarian parent who cannot allow "his children" to grow up and become self-defining, self-actualizing adults. The relationship of children to parents, wives to husbands, laity to ministers, and subjects to rulers perpetuates a certain infantilism when these authority figures are seen to represent "God" in this way. In order to affirm the absoluteness of God, one denies the capacity of the "creaturely" will to do anything "of itself" other than sin. All positive action is imposed on the self from outside itself by God, in whose hands the "creature" is either a passive vehicle of election or is in revolt. Any affirmation of the self is seen as detracting from divine sovereignty.

The Christ-church relationship has often been seen as a duplicate of this hierarchical, God-creature relationship, and this, in turn, has become a renewed sanction for similar relationships in the church, in society, and in the family. Christ is the lord and master who sanctions the subjugation of the body and creation to the commanding "head," the subjugation of wives to husband, people to priest, bishop and pope, slaves to masters, subjects to rulers. The subjugation of women to men is particularly important in this concept of relationship in active-passive terms. In spite of frequent references to Buber's concept of "I-Thou" as the model for self-God and self-self relations in recent Christian theology, the dominant model for these relationships in Christian theology is actually an I-it or subject-object, rather than subject-subject model. The messiah image has its roots in the concept of a warrior-king, who is the son-delegate of the sovereign Father; images deeply rooted in political mastery. As Logos, the Christ image draws on the mind-body duality of Greek philosophy that saw the body as either passive instrument or dangerous rebel against the sovereignty of the mind over the "flesh."

The primary image of Christ and the church draws on the male-dominant-female-submission model of marriage. The church as bride of Christ is passive, obedient and asexual. She is a virgin bride whose womb gives rebirth to souls through a virginal conception that overcomes the tainting sexual conception by which actual humans are born to mortality and sin from the wombs of real mothers. The church as virgin mother (personalized in Mary) represents the "good feminine," in contrast to "bad femaleness." Bad femaleness is the creaturely will identified especially with sexuality in revolt against the mastery of the sovereign mind. Femaleness in its "natural state" is sin. Good femininity, on the other hand, represents the creaturely as passive vehicle of divine male will. While males can participate in both sides of this active-passive relationship, experiencing themselves as "feminine" in relation to God and Christ, but as the representative of the "divine masculine" as husband, clergy, or leaders, women are allowed, symbolically and socially, only the negative or dependent underside of this relationship.

The authoritarian, active-passive model structures all relationship along sado-masochistic lines. The self is "nothing" in relation to whatever authority is "above," and "everything" in relation to whatever subject is "below." Activity and leadership is construed as domination that must reduce the "other" to powerless acceptance of being acted-upon. Recent psychoanalysis and religious symbolism have tried to overcome the polarization of this male-female, active-passive split by insisting that Christ is androgynous and that every self is ultimately androgynous, combining "male" and "female" characteristics. This is an important step toward wholeness, but it is not sufficient. If "maleness" and "femaleness" are simply brought together in a composite picture of the self, but the characteristics of each are still viewed on active-passive lines, one simply integrates into one person the same hierarchical model of the self. Such androgyny is inevitably androcentric, for the "male" still represents the principle of the directing self. This puts women into a contradictory situation. However much there may be an insistence that they too are androgynous, the role suggested for them is still the auxiliary "nurturance" of the underside of a selfhood that can appear in its wholeness only in male persons. They are always the muse and mother to a hero-trip whose representative is male.

There are, I believe, in Christianity alternatives to this active-passive model of divine-human, inter- and intra-human relations. One can look at God as source of being, not as sovereign ego over against dependent object, but as the matrix or ground of being out of which the self springs and is constantly renewed. This is a gestational, participatory, rather than externalized, tool-making image of divine-human relationship. This model of God as divine ground does not create a hierarchical polarity between God and nature, nature and grace, immanence and transcendence. Nature is founded upon and constantly renewed in divine grace. God as divine ground is not a divinization of present existence, but the depth of being as a transcendent possibility of fullness of being that is both the true and the new humanity. The divine matrix is the inexhaustible source of life out of which we constantly *become*. God as "thou" is the foundation rather than the authoritarian negation of the "thouness" of every person. The sexist hierarchical model is dissolved for a process model of God as the moving dialectic of being. The God of transcendent newness is not set over against creation. Rather, the renewal of the world is the continual re-establishment of that authentic existence in divine fullness through which the world is created. This process model of God and creation relates nature and spirit, free will and grace in a dynamic and participatory, rather than polarized way that is characteristic of Western theology. Nature is founded on and expressive of divine gift. One's deepest self-actualization and activity are at the same time one's fullness, grounding upon the divine being which is the root of authentic life. God is not the neurotic parent that makes us nothing so the "he" can be everything, but God is the empowering Spirit that founds our freedom for self-actualization.

The Christ-church relationship likewise might be understood in a different way more consonant with kenotic and incarnational theology. For this we must draw upon the antihierarchicalism and iconoclastic side of Jesus' teachings as a model for the role of Christ to humanity. Jesus' model of community seems to have been one in which the hierarchy of domination and subjugation is replaced by a community of brothers and sisters related to each other in mutual service. The leaders of the community are called to renounce power roles and emulate the role of Christ of self-spending in service.

> You know that the rulers of the Gentiles lord it over them and their great men exercise authority over them. But it shall not be so among you; but whoever would be great among you must be your servant . . . even as the Son of Man came not to be served, but to serve and to give his life as ransom for many.
>
> Matthew 20: 25–27

The radical character of this kenotic model of relationship has often been lost in Christianity by confusing service with servitude and thus making salvation through service a way of reaffirming the traditional servitude of women and slaves, while mystifying the lordship of the new Christian leaders by calling their princely power and domination "ministry." Service implies autonomy and power, but used in behalf of others, liberating and empowering others for true selfhood. Jesus called his disciples to service and made Christ the model of service; he did not reify the servitude of women or slaves. On the contrary, the kenosis of divine power that makes itself a servant at the same time calls the oppressed out of servitude and makes them members and indeed the paradigmatic "heads" of the new liberated humanity. In this great reversal and conversion to redeemed humanity, the prostitutes and beggars will go ahead of *you*—the proud leaders of institutionalized authority—into the kingdom of God.

In Christ we might even say that God is "dealienated." The image of God as alienated sovereign ego is overcome as God grasps no longer at exalted station, but "empties himself and becomes a servant." We might say that in the kenosis of Christ the modeling of divine transcendence after male, leadership-class domination is overcome by God! God becomes the empowering Spirit. Thereby all leadership is enjoined to cease to be "masters" who reduce others to being tools of their will, and to become servants empowering others. The poor women, in turn are called to come forth out of their servitude to become disciples, to become equals as brothers and sisters. Martha is rebuked for being "too much occupied with serving" in the sense of the traditional female role. Mary's claim to participation in the circle of disciples is affirmed as the "better part" (Luke 10: 38–42). Mary, at the incarnation, becomes the voice of the messianic community in whom God does mighty things: the proud are scattered in the imagination of their heart; the mighty are put down from their thrones; those of low degree are exalted; the poor are filled with good things (Luke 1:50–55).

Kenotic christology does not exalt a new lord that can be a role model for new lords of power and domination in society. Neither does it bring together both sides of a master-subject relationship in a hierarchical "complementarity." Rather, it is a christology and ecclesiology of conversion and transformation. Alienated power is overcome. Those who presently have and represent such power are called to lay down this power in service or to be overthrown. The subjugated are lifted up. They lead the way into the inheritance of the earth in the liberated kingdom of redemption. The last of the present system are first; the first last. God no longer supports domination, but is poured out into creation to overcome oppression. Women, the poor, slaves are liberated from servitude. This is a christology of process; the process of creating a new humanity of wholeness of self in community.

This kenotic, conversionist model of Christ and the messianic people suggests a similar conversionist concept as the model of redeemed selfhood, redeemed relation to others. One cannot identify with a "feminine" receptivity linked to powerless dependency. Nor with a "male" activism linked to domination that reduces others to subjugation. This is why it is insufficient to bring together both sides into an "androgyny" that preserves the hierarchical model of self and social relations. One must dissolve and transform both sides of the false dualism, psychically and socially. Receptivity is possible only for the person of autonomy and self-esteem. Activity is freed from domination only when put at the service of the empowerment of others. This is a revolution of relationship that is suggested by Jesus' concept of ministry.

Women today are claiming their own discipleship in the messianic new creation, and in so doing rejecting the patriarchicalism in which it was traditionally cast. Not only must women be empowered to think and act as full persons, and men be put in touch with their receptive and nurturing powers, but the way in which these processes were related to each other must be transformed, so that activity is no longer a function of domination and receptivity no longer a function of dependency. This is the fallen humanity which makes our power barren and our openness craven. We seek instead a mutuality and reciprocity that creates self-actualization by the same process by which we put ourselves at the disposal of others. This implies not just a change of consciousness, but a change of power relations, a recreation of the social structures by which women and men, rich and poor are related to each other. The hierarchical polarization of the human psyche into power-ego maleness and receptive-emotive femininity can only be overcome when the power-dependency relations, which these symbols were created to sanctify, cease to characterize society. This is not "unisex" or monolithic "grey," but the flowering of individuality in community released from sexist, classist reductionism.

Theologically this vision of transformatory process is called redemption. It is the reconciliation of humanity with itself; the reconciliation of people with each other, and humanity with nature. The reconciliation of creation with itself is the visible revelation of the reconciliation of humanity with God. But humanity can be reconciled with God only when the patriarchal "God" is converted to become the ground of mutuality in the world. The death of God the Father is the overthrowing of the alienated image of male egoism projected into heaven which sanctifies all relations of domination and subjugation in creation. The kenosis of God is the ground of the appearance of the new messianic covenant of creation. This is that new creation glimpsed, but unrealizable under the patriarchal form of the gospel. The risen Christ goes ahead of us as representative of the unrealized new humanity and new creation for which we still search and long; that new humanity in which "the dividing wall of hostility has been broken down to reconcile those who have been alienated from one another" (Ephesians 2:14).

CHAPTER 11

A PROCESS/DEVELOPMENTAL VIEW OF THE DIVINE/HUMAN RELATIONSHIP

Howard Grimes

Both process theology and a systematic view of human development are relatively recent emergents in human thought. Neither is really new, however, although both have been formulated in more precise theoretical terms in the twentieth century. Biblical theology, in fact, seems more compatible with process metaphysics than with that of classical theism, whose framework is Platonic amd Aristotelian philosophy. The nurturing process commanded in Deuteronomy 6:4-9 and supported in principle by Jesus in his dealing with children (Matthew 19:13-15, Mark 10:13-16, and Luke 18:15-17) is a tacit recognition of the uniqueness of the young. Theology, especially in its more experiential forms, has never lost the biblical view of the dynamic character of God, and various movements, especially during the nineteenth century, reaffirmed the importance of accepting children as children, not "little adults." It is now possible, however, to relate a dynamic view of God with human development in a more ordered manner. The purpose of this chapter, therefore, is to advance in a modest way the thesis that process theology and developmental psychology complement each other in understanding the divine/human relationship.

PROCESS THEOLOGY

Although the reality of God is not the only interest of process theologians, it is at the center of their concern.[1] Further, God's relationship with the created order, especially persons, is the focus, a fact illustrated especially by Daniel Day Williams' *The Spirit and the Forms of Love*. In this regard, as well as in other matters, they reflect the biblical emphasis, for in the Bible God is understood as a covenant-making God who enters into relationships with humanity in a creating and saving manner. The covenant with Noah is with all living creatures (Genesis 9:8–17); with Abraham it is with a special nation through whom "all the families of the earth shall be blessed" (Genesis 12:3, alternate reading). To Moses the promise is that "you shall be to me a kingdom of priests and a holy nation" (Exodus 19:6). The prophetic writings stress God's relational activity, as in Hosea 11 and Jeremiah 31:31–34. In Jesus as the Christ the "new covenant" is made, with the Lord's Supper as sign and seal (1 Corinthians 11:25).

Systematic theologians and ordinary Christians of varying theological persuasions, however, have tended to superimpose upon the dynamic understanding of God in the Bible the static notion of "immutable being," which the early church fathers borrowed from Platonic and Aristotelian metaphysics. If, as Schubert Ogden has pointed out, God is understood as the "barren absolute" (as in classical metaphysics), then he is "by definition related to nothing," but instead, in Christian understanding, God is "related to everything." God's absolute character is preserved, however, and consists of his "being related to all others" and thus "relative to nothing," "the absolute ground of any and all relationships, whether his own or those of his creatures."[2] Or as John Cobb puts it, God "is the lover of the world" "who calls it ever beyond what it has attained to affirming life, novelty, consciousness, and freedom again and again."[3] God's love, as Williams reminds us, is seen supremely in the cross where Jesus reveals "the love which does not shirk suffering, and that love is God himself at work."[4]

To use my own terms, "dynamic becoming" rather than "immutable being" seems to be most clearly the way in which the Christian understanding of God can be expressed. Jesus' use of the word "Father" for God, although now in disfavor in some circles because of its exclusively male orientation, has been an important factor that has kept Christian piety from fully accepting classical metaphysics. The element of judgment

is by no means omitted from such an understanding; the father
in Luke's parable waits until the prodigal makes his own decision
to return home, and there is a poignant mixture of love and
judgment as the father speaks to the pouting elder brother. The
love of God is not sentimentality but active good-will, which
seeks the well-being of human creatures without compulsion.
Further, in Luke's parable, the father's love both understands
and adjusts to the peculiar situation of the two brothers, and by
analogy we can assume that Jesus so understood God's love. It is
at this point that developmental psychology provides meaningful data for understanding the nature of the divine/human relationship, and to that phase of this essay we now turn.

DEVELOPMENTAL PSYCHOLOGY

It is patently unfair to picture all those who related to children prior to the modern period as treating them like "little
adults." In Western civilization, however—more so than in
primitive cultures—the *tendency* has been to think of children as
"preparing to be adults." As formal education became more
common during the nineteenth century, schools were usually
understood to be a "preparation for life," a condition against
which John Dewey in particular reacted. In more recent times
an opposite extreme has developed so that our culture is often
interpreted as a child- and youth-dominated one. Actually
neither of these extremes is compatible with a developmental
approach to understanding the person. If the person is more
accurately denoted by the word "becoming" rather than by "being,"[5] each stage of development can be seen as having a basic
integrity of its own.

Developmental psychology has a long history and many ad-
vocates, but no one has contributed more to contemporary
theory than the Swiss "genetic epistemologist" Jean Piaget.[6]
There are problems associated with any theory which posits
clearly defined "stages of development," and Piaget's theory
and research have the additional problem of being concerned
primarily with cognitive development. The stages no doubt
blend into one another and may not be nearly so exact as they
are often thought to be. I believe them to be useful constructs,

however, and, further, that the stage theory as developed by the contemporary theorist and researcher James W. Fowler has particular relevance for understanding the divine/human relationship.

Fowler, whose work is still in progress and by his admission not fully verified by empirical evidence, has drawn from the prior work of Piaget, Erik Erikson, and Lawrence Kohlberg.[7] Influenced also by H. Richard Niebuhr, Fowler has posited six stages of faith development, related to and partly dependent on Piaget's stages of cognitive development and Erikson's more affectively oriented "ages of the person." Fowler's stages are also similar to but not identical with Kohlberg's stages of moral development.

Fowler is concerned *not* with the content but the *structure* of faith-knowing, a combination of the cognitive and the affective. "Faith is a knowing which includes loving, caring and valuing, as well as awe, dread and fear," he writes.[8] His interest is in all forms of faith—any "human relatedness to the Transcendent." Each of the six stages is seen as a structural whole, consisting of "the pattern of operations or modes of thinking and valuing which are constitutive of the person's ability to use and give form to beliefs, values, ideas and propositions."[9]

The six stages, briefly noted, are as follows, with the *minimum* age indicated for each stage. Stage 1 involves an imitation of others (age 4). Stage 2 is that which involves the mythic and the literal (ages 6½–8). Stage 3 represents a time when the authority of others is accepted (ages 12–13). Stage 4 begins with the acceptance of responsibility for one's own commitments, lifestyle, beliefs, and attitudes, a time of individuation and differentiation (ages 18–19). Stage 5 involves the holding of one's own commitments with a recognition of the value of those of others (ages 30–32). Stage 6 is that of the rare individual who participates directly in the ultimate (ages 38–40).[10]

Fowler has found in his interviews that a position between Stages 3 and 4 is the most common among his adult interviewees,[11] and Gerald Calhoun, using Fowler's stages and methodology with schizophrenic adults, found all of his subjects to be in either Stages 2 or 3.[12] Fowler does not assign value to the stages, insisting rather that "each stage describes a pat-

tern of valuing, thinking, feeling, and committing which is potentially worthy, serene, and 'graceful.' "[13]

SOME CONCLUSIONS AND SOME QUESTIONS

I shall draw three conclusions concerning the way in which
process theology illuminates the meaning of the divine/human
relationship as seen from the perspective of Fowler's stages of
faith development. The first grows out of the point made in the
previous paragraph and sustains Fowler in his insistence that
there is a kind of integrity about each of the six stages. The
problem which is basic to this conclusion is the fact that the New
Testament understanding of faith, especially in Paul, seems to
be a condition at least equivalent to Stage 4 and perhaps even
nearer Stage 5.

If God is understood to be a "static absolute," then one may
conclude that a right relationship with God is dependent upon
a particular understanding of faith, a common assertion in
Protestant theology. On the other hand, when God is understood as "dynamic becoming"—who is both cause and effect,
that is, is responsive to people in terms of who *they* are[14]—then
God's relationship with a person is *not* dependent on a particular condition of the human respondent, even a "proper understanding" of faith. The Stage 3 person, for example, who finds
it necessary for his faith to be objectified by a human agent
(such as a charismatic leader), a book (such as the Bible), or a set
of rules (legalism), can know God meaningfully for the very
reason that Paul discovered at his Stage 5 understanding experience of faith; namely, that it is God's initiative that makes
faith possible, not human striving or human achievement (even
the attainment of a particular level of faith-understanding).

This does not solve the *human* problem of the temptation to
make one's own perceptions normative. According to Fowler,
Stage 5 persons are able, within limits, to appreciate the faith-
responses of persons at "lower" stages. It is perhaps this attitude which one sees in Paul's struggle both to appreciate the
Law and at the same time to lead others beyond legalism (Stage
3) to an individuated and differentiated faith (Stage 4). Further, we can be less anxious over the fact that children do not

have the ability to respond as adults, and recognize that the adult who seeks a religious response from the child must do so in terms of that child's own faith development. If God relates to persons in this manner, then it must also be part of the human struggle to do so.

The second implication, which grows jointly out of developmental psychology and process theology, pertains to the lack of abstract reasoning ("formal operations" in Piaget's terms) prior to middle adolescence. Classical theism, especially in its Protestant versions, has usually made *rational understanding* the condition of a faith response. When God is seen as the immutable absolute, this may well be the logical inference, since this view of God tends to exalt reason above love. God as dynamic becoming should not be understood to be *irrational,* however, nor even *non*rational, but rather as outgoing love and therefore *trans*rational and willing to relate to creatures in ways other than the rational.

In actual practice we have recognized the importance of the relational aspect of teaching, especially of younger children. Often, however, our more pressing concern has been to find ways by which religious truth can be interpreted to children in terms of *their level of understanding.*[15] Bible stories are therefore simplified so that the child can *understand* them, and we have often failed to realize that a child can *feel* a story even when it is not understood. So with faith, as Fowler presents it: it is not dependent solely on rational understanding. While there is a danger that we may undervalue the rational aspect of faith if we press this point too far, Fowler's holding in tension of the cognitive and the affective is a deterrent to an antiintellectualism.

The third implication is a complex one and grows out of the viewing of the entire life cycle as developmental. Erikson's final stage ("integrity vs. despair"),[16] Maslow's "self-actualization,"[17] and Fowler's Stage 6 are rather remarkably alike, and what all of them say sounds very much like the Christian doctrine of sanctification or Christian perfection at its best. "Perfectionists" have tended to miss the meaning of Christian perfection because they see it in static rather than dynamic terms. If God is understood as the immutable absolute, I suppose some such view of a "state to be attained" is the logical inference. If, on the other hand, God is a dynamic becoming—and love is always dynamic—then the "final" stages of Erikson, Maslow, and Fowler, and Christian perfection all are quite the opposite of perfect rule-keeping and instead become the expression of perfect love. And this is precisely what John Wesley, who emphasized Christian perfection more than any other major church leader, understood by Christian perfection—as "loving God with all our heart, mind, soul, and strength" so that "all the thoughts, words, and actions are governed by pure love."[18]

Understanding God as dynamic becoming solves the problem of the integrity of persons in stages of faith development other than that in which *faith alone in God* is the central reality. It also provides the basis for perceiving a child—or a mentally retarded adult—as able to respond to God because God, as it were, "adjusts" to meet the need of that person. And it provides new insights concerning both the possibility and the nature of "going on to perfection." It does not solve the problem of how a Stage 5 person relates to one on Stage 3, nor how an adult who is rationally oriented can sufficiently concretize the teaching provided for a six-year-old to elicit a faith response of which that child is capable. Nor does it answer the question of how the church leader, or parent, can help the child move more expeditiously from one stage to another, and it in particular does not answer the question of both the responsibility and the methodology for encouraging adults to move from Stage 3 through Stage 4 to Stage 5, and perhaps even begin to glimpse the possibilities of what it means to be a self-actualized person in relation to God. We have usually depended on some exterior crisis as catalysis for growth in faith, and when we have contrived such a crisis (as in an advanced Bible course which seeks to destroy bibliolatry), we have not usually followed through from the crisis to a more integrated faith-response.

CONCLUSION

I have just begun to suggest the possibilities in relating process theology and developmental psychology, and in doing so have raised as many questions as I have tried to answer. The purpose of the essay has been only to suggest the fruitful union

of these two twentieth-century developments. I believe, however, that I have said enough to indicate that there are exciting
possibilities in this relationship for improving the theory and
practice of the church's effort in communicating faith to those
both within and outside the organized church.

Notes

1. A brief introduction to the development of this kind of theological think-
   ing is found in Norman Pittenger's *Process-Thought and Christian Faith,*
   The Macmillan Company, 1968. A more extensive discussion of the
   movement is contained in Randolph Crump Miller's *The American Spirit in
   Theology,* United Church Press, 1974, Chaps. 8–11. Alfred North
   Whitehead's final chapter in *Process and Reality,* The Macmillan Company, 1929) contains a clear statement of the triumph of Greek and
   Roman philosophy over biblical theology in the early centuries of the
   church.
2. Schubert M. Ogden, *The Reality of God,* Harper & Row, 1966, pp. 59–60.
3. John B. Cobb, Jr., *God and the World,* The Westminster Press, 1969, p. 65.
4. Daniel Day Williams, *The Spirit and the Forms of Love,* Harper & Row, 1968,
   p. 185.
5. Cf. Gordon W. Allport, *Becoming,* Yale University Press, 1955, especially
   Section 5.
6. For a summary of Piaget's theory, see *The Psychology of the Child* by Jean
   Piaget and Bärbell Inhelder, trans. Helen Weaver, Basic Books, 1969. See
   also Ruth M. Beard, *An Outline of Piaget's Developmental Psychology for
   Students and Teachers,* Basic Books, 1969.
7. See the works of Erikson and Kohlberg.
8. James W. Fowler, "Faith, Liberation and Human Development," *The
   Foundation* (Published by Gammon Theological Seminary, Atlanta, Georgia), Vol. LXXIX, No. 10 (Spring, 1974), p. 8.
9. I have quoted from a mimeographed article by James Fowler, "Stages in
   Faith: The Structural-Developmental Approach," p. 14.
10. The two published articles in which the six stages are described are
    "Faith, Liberation and Human Development," op. cit., and "Toward a
    Developmental Perspective on Faith," *Religious Education,* LXIX: 207–19
    (March-April, 1974).
11. Stages in Faith" (mimeographed version), op. cit., p. 11.
12. Gerald J. Calhoun, "An Analysis of the Faith Development in a Select
    Group of Schizophrenics," unpublished doctor of ministry project, Per-
    kins School of Theology, Southern Methodist University, 1976, p. 118.
13. James W. Fowler, "Stages in Faith" (mimeographed version), op. cit., p.
    18.
14. Schubert M. Ogden, "Toward a New Theism," in *The Credibility of God,*
    Muskingum College, 1967, pp. 15–6.
15. For example, the basic assumption of Ronald Goldman in his research
    using Piaget's methodology to study religious readiness in children and
    adolescents seems to be cognitive understanding as the principal factor.

See *Religious Thinking from Childhood to Adolescence,* The Seabury Press, 1964, and *Readiness for Religion,* The Seabury Press, 1970.

16. Erik H. Erikson, *Childhood and Society,* Second Edition, W. W. Norton & Company, 1963), pp. 268–9 and *Identity: Youth and Crisis,* W. W. Norton & Company, 1968, pp. 139–41.

17. A brief discussion of Maslow's basic needs is found in A. H. Maslow, "A Theory of Human Motivation: The Basic Needs," in *Organizational Behavior and The Practice of Management,* ed. David R. Hampton, Charles E. Summer, and Ross A. Webber, Scott, Foresman and Company, 1968, pp. 27–40.

18. "Thoughts on Christian Perfection," (1759), in *John Wesley,* ed. Albert C. Outler, Oxford University Press, 1964, p. 284.

CHAPTER 12

THE IMPERATIVE DIALOGUE

Reuel L. Howe

All meaning is discovered in dialogue: whether it is an inner dialogue with the self or a dialogue with nature, dialogue with another, or dialogue with God.

God becomes remote and unreal and our relationship with him and others lacks depth and excitement and fails to grow because our dialogue is often impeded or blocked altogether by limitations imposed by us.

If I will not address and respond, I cannot know myself or another. And the same is true for any partner, and also for my relationship with God. Where there is no mutual communication, there can be no growth of relationship. The relationship of God and man depends on the process of dialogue.

The scriptures are, among other things, a record of the dialogue between God and his people in which it is evident that God not only addresses them but expects response from them. Scripture is a record of his people's response expressed in both word and action. Scripture also reveals that God is influenced by his people's responses: their actions, sufferings, and joys.

The quality and intensity of the dialogue between God and his people varies. There is evidence that the greater the faith the more vigorous and real is the dialogue. When human trust is weak the human part of the dialogue becomes more tentative, defensive, and characterized by fear. Working with people and their faith-responses indicates that much of their side of the dialogue with God is guarded, largely because they do not feel that God can take the frankness of their feelings, especially their negative ones. In much religious expression there is an obvious attempt to put the best foot forward, to cover up their

91

doubt, distrust, anger, and fear. Our relationship with God is often lived defensively and protectingly and is consistent with the way we live with our fellow human beings. In other words courage in a relationship with God is frequently conspicuously absent. When there is no honest dialogue there is impaired relationship, and God has to relate to people who are too defensive to relate.

Equally defeating of dialogue is the attitude of looking to God for literal direction in everything they do. Such people regard God as their own private entrepreneur. Such an expectation creates a complete dependency on God accompanied by an abdication of responsibility for their decisions and actions. This kind of believer is mindless, compliant, and passive. "I had this terrible decision to make but I just told God about it and he told me what to do. I did it and everything is fine." Or, "I have never been without an answer. By either sign or word, I've been told what I should do." Even a human parent would get tired of this kind of child, especially after he had reached forty years of age! That's not childlike, it's childish, since it reveals a lack of maturity, autonomy, initiative, and courage. This attitude and expectation ignores the whole principle of incarnation; since God desires to speak, act, and love through his people's power to speak, act, and love. Human power is always vulnerable power, but the vulnerable power of the spirit of the crucified one seeks to use our vulnerable power to accomplish his purposes. The Holy Spirit in our own time seeks to interact with the human spirit and looks to the human spirit for interactive embodiment.

Our spiritual growth, which really means a maturing relationship with God and man, requires vigor, intellectual and emotional freedom, and determination. Our potential dialogue with God is beautifully represented in many passages of the Psalms and in the prayers and sayings of Jesus, especially his exclamations from the cross; their ruggedness reveals the gutlessness of much that passes for human devotion. Often when I listen to prayers that are prayed in church, I wonder who the pray-er thinks he is kidding.

My first sense of the stalwartness of human participation in partnership with God was experienced when, as a young boy,

I heard my mother say that she fully expected that she would be asked many questions when she appeared before the throne of grace, but, she added, "I have a lot of questions to ask, too."

Another nondialogical concept of God is the subhuman one. God is a projection of people who impute to him their own likes, dislikes, prejudices, and other limitations. Out of their need, he becomes like the people who believe in him and from him they receive confirmation of what they are. There is no challenge in the relationship and therefore no change. He becomes the God of the status quo. Many of them fill the pews of our churches, but when they attend they filter the radical good news through their "status quoism" and "one-wayism." God is actor and wants a two-way relationship.

I borrow from Randolph Crump Miller the phrase: "God is what God does." Scripture accords that God's revelation has to do with events and not propositions. We therefore look for him in action, in creation, and in the processes of becoming and perishing. The gospel is good news from God through Christ to people in specific situations of fear, loneliness, sin, and confusion. It is the good news of the action of God in our behalf. St. Paul described that action: "God was in Christ reconciling the world unto himself." The word "reconciliation" is just right because the human condition is one of alienation. He seeks to do this reconciling work through his people. "Therefore, if anyone is in Christ, he is a new creation." We are "ambassadors of Christ, God making his appeal through us." God is that process by which we are made new, strengthened, directed, comforted, forgiven, and saved, and by which we are lured into feelings of wonder, awe, and reverence.

We meet God out of our struggle and pilgrimage. Every experience of life has in it the possibilities for alienation, destruction, and death; and also for reconciliation, fulfillment, and life. Every human situation is one in which there is tension between life and death. This means that our situation is never so good that we are not the victims of demonic forces working both in us and on us, nor so bad that there are not the possibilities of life and redemption.

Nowhere are there conflicting possibilities more clear than in the eight fundamental and crucial experiences of human life:

birth, growth, maturity, mating (or lack of it), parenthood, sickness and other crises (unemployment, loss of money), bereavement, and death. These are the common ventures of life to which all are called and to which, if they live, they must make some kind of response.

Each of these holds promise of life and death for all of us. Birth, for instance, which seems to suggest only the possibility of life is commonly referred to as a "blessed event," but have we not seen times when it set parents against each other? If a child is not wanted or not wanted for the right reason, his birth may be an occasion of separation, destruction, and death. Many people wish they had never been born. This can only mean that the birth of such a person was far from being a blessed event and was instead more destructive than life-giving. Or here is a couple coming in love and with hope to their marriage. Will this experience be one that will produce a growing sense of communion and union or will they come to know chiefly loneliness and anxiety? In all of these common experiences of persons we see the promise of life and death.

We think of these experiences as times of crisis when we must make decisions. Back of decisions are the great, fundamental questions that lie deep in our experiences of which we may not be aware. They are ontological questions because they grow out of and are concerned for our *being*, like "Who am I?" "Who are you?" "How can I become who I am?" "What shall I do with the life I have?" "Is there a love that can survive and overcome the alienation that is inevitable in all human relationships?" etc. These questions and variations of them are shaped with varying degrees of clarity. Most ontological questions are not asked by us verbally but nonverbally, by our actions, lifestyles, and events that we cause.

To what and to whom are these questions directed? Because they are questions having to do with our being they are directed, whether we are aware of it or not, to the source of all being, God. And God's action is his response to the human question.

The arena for this dialogue between people and God is, of course, the world. Thus the world has collaborative meaning for human beings, for God, for the church, and for the individual. What, then, does this world mean to man and to God.

1. For man the world is an arena for self-actualization.
2. For God the world is an arena for self-revelation.
3. The world is the sphere of the church's mission.
4. The world is the testing ground of the individual's profession of faith.

First, the world for us is an arena for self-actualization. It is a place where achievements and failures are experienced in personal, family, industrial, and political life; where the expanding frontiers of the physical and social sciences are explored; where we grapple with the destiny of the race in all aspects of human existence.

People find their values in the world. These values become incarnate in their decisions and give power to their commitments, whether to life or death, to God or the demonic. We must remember that we are always giving to and withholding ourselves from something or someone, often without knowing to whom or to what. Unfortunately, many men and women are led by the church to say "yes" to Christ without knowing what it means to say "yes" to him, or that in so doing they should be saying "no" to other things and values. Both their "yea" and "nay" are vague and unclear.

The struggle between races and between nations holding conflicting values has ontological as well as sociological and political meaning, and cannot be understood apart from those meanings. Deep questions are raised by men and women as they face and fight their issues in life's arena. The world, therefore, is to be taken seriously and its life understood if we would be responsible leaders in the name of Christ.

It is imperative, therefore, that we be observant and take time to ask individuals and organizations about themselves, their purposes, and their questions before we presume to teach them. How can we tell them what the good news is unless we and they know in the terms of our own lives what is our specific need for the gospel? Many of the frustrations experienced by ministers are due to their failures to listen to the world before they speak. All of us need to remember that proclamation of the gospel calls for use of ears as well as mouth, and not by mouth alone. We must first remember to listen with the gospel before we seek to proclaim it. We must listen with the spirit and the understanding of Christ, and out of that speak.

Second, the world for God is an arena for self-revelation. The gospel is co-active with the dynamics of human life. God revealed himself in the same world in which human beings find themselves. God in Christ entered the arena of the world where he participated as a man in human life. By this act he sought to break us out of the vicious ambiguity of love and hate and give us power as persons to be human in a new way. The world, then, is not only a place where we seek to actualize ourselves, but also where God actualized himself as human in order that we might realize ourselves as we were created to be: reconciled and reunited to ourselves, to our fellows, and to our God.

Now we see the world as the object of God's love; a place where he is accomplishing his purposes; where he found and lived with us, and where we were met by and lived with him. And now his spirit lives and works in the world, drawing us to Christ through our struggles, questions, experiments, and devotions. As he fully revealed himself in the world and not in the synagogue or temple, so we will find him by living responsibly in the world.

Third, the world, therefore, is where the church must realize itself as a church, where its main concern is for life, not religion. Religion is only a resource to guide and enable persons to find in their relations with one another their union with God. The world does not exist for the church; the church was sent into the world to incarnate in the life of the world the spirit of Christ.

Fourth, the world is a testing-ground for individuals. Persons are a primary "means of grace," a means by which God acts in the world, a means of introducing into the structures of living a vitality that may reform and transform them. The gospel both judges and affirms us. The world, therefore, is the testing-ground of our use of the gifts of life and of God's forgiveness. If the effect of our decision and action is reconciliation, then we have passed the test: we *have* forgiven because we *are* forgiven.

Individuals need more training in accepting forgiveness and in forgiving.

We are judged in every encounter, decision, and action in which we participate, but these same encounters, decisions, and actions may also become occasions for grace; times when we are confronted by God and his love and truth, and may know and accept his forgiveness. Every meaning of life, no matter how small and casual it may be, has a relation to ultimate meaning: "Inasmuch as you have done it unto the least of these, you have done it unto me." When we discriminate against any person we act against the reconciling God. And every true act of love participates in God's reconciling work.

The world is a testing ground also in the sense that out of its life come the honest questions that move men and women nearer the truth. The "answers" we would give require their questions in order that answers may be recognized as such. Instead of thrusting answers at people, the ministry of reconciliation is one that helps persons raise the questions that, when asked, become a first step in breaking down the walls that separate person from person and group from group.

Our task is to listen to the world, to hear its questions and concerns, then speak out of the gospel that which is relevant. Because we believe that God is already at work in the world, we believe that he directs the church and guides its responses to the world by shaping the formulation of the world's questions and challenges. Attention to the world, then, is attention given to God who works in the world through historical movements. The dialogue is between God speaking and acting through men and women in church and God speaking and acting through men and women in the world, in which dialogue we may all be participants in both identities.

Our relationship with God is one of continuing process that depends on a relationship of open and honest dialogue. Dialogue with God requires:

1. That we accept our dependence upon his love, and our need to love in turn.

2. Being also independent in relation to him. He will not do for us what we can do for ourselves. This means that we must

accept what we can do for ourselves: to think, decide and act; to suffer without comfort; to love and forgive even when we don't want to; to be lost but still pursue our pilgrimage.

3. Being open to the living God: changeless and yet ever changing; open to the different ways he may act and to the relationship he may offer.

4. Being in dialogue with ourselves and with others.

5. Risking our being in dialogue with ourselves and with others.

6. Asking hard questions and avoiding easy answers. It means hammering at the door of meaning until it opens.

7. Being aware of our positive and negative feelings and honest in our expression of them.

8. Letting God be free of the yoke of our religious convictions and prejudices even as he has freed us from the legalisms of religion. It means resisting the temptation to imprison him in our sanctuaries.

9. Being alert and responsive to the meanings implicit in the events of human life.

Honest and open dialogue is not easy. But the rewards for accomplishing it are unmatched. Once we have experienced the depth of this kind of dialogue, it becomes imperative for our living together.

CHAPTER 13

REVELATION AND THE LIFE CYCLE

Donald E. Miller

The task of contemporary theology is to find a way between empiricism and formalism. Traditional formalism searched for the deep and abiding structures that organize human life. Whether it was Plato's "eternal forms" or Kant's "synthetic a priori," the effort to find the unchanging patterns of human life remained essentially the same.

Theologically, formalism is an effort to find the unchanging plan of God behind all the changes of human life. Whether we speak of God's eternal laws or of God's plans predestined from before the creation, the conception is much the same. Medieval theology made a remarkable effort to characterize the eternal plan of God. Calvinism spoke of God's predestined plan, but acknowledged that we have only a most imperfect grasp of it. The gap between our knowledge and God's plan is filled by our faith that all is to the glory of God.

The tendency that opposes formalism is empiricism. Since the Renaissance the modern world has become increasingly confident about empirical experience. We hardly need illustrate how the modern sciences have grown out of the careful and disciplined study of empirical events. Perhaps Hume was the most thoroughgoing empiricist. He declared that there is no necessary or substantial connection between any one event and another. The connections are supplied by associations in the human mind. We associate the striking of a match with the flame, and so we say the one causes the other. What we actually mean is that in our experience the one has been associated with the other many times. The association is habitual or customary, but not "really" there.

Empiricism has influenced theology in many ways. Luther's principle of "justification by faith" can lead one to the eternal plan of God, but it has often served to lead people to accept the unceasing change of life. A theology of dialogue may lead one to God's laws of communication, but more often it points to an I-Thou relationship that may fit equally well in all circumstances. Historicism in theology gives an account of changing doctrines and beliefs. The historical method in biblical studies attempts to locate the events of the times and the motives of the author as a way of discovering the meaning of the text. Process theology usually sacrifices God's foreknowledge and power in order to stress God's empathy and concern for people as they face the actual anxiety and pain of life.

Both formalism and empiricism fail as theological methods. Formalism fails because every past attempt to characterize the eternal laws of God turn out in a later century to be very inadequate. There is no reason to think that our efforts will be more successful than those of previous generations. Empiricism fails because it delivers all life to an extreme relativism that is unable to give us guidance or comfort. The revelation of "the moment" may cover fathoms of anxiety, but it delivers us to a life of "leaps" and impulses. When equally competent scholars using the same methods date the exodus as much as a thousand years apart, then the historical method is failing to give us guidance. When God's love becomes sympathy without firmness, or when revelation becomes an ecstatic experience for each person in his or her own way, then the guidance of both God's love and God's revelation has been lost. Something beyond both formalism or empiricism is needed.

In my judgment the most hopeful direction for theology is with those methods that search for structures which are dynamic and transformational.[1] Our effort becomes one of searching for patterns and regularities in human life, rather than being content with trust, empathy, or dialogue in the midst of change. There are structural elements in biblical thought that cannot be dismissed by historical studies. The exodus is an account of human interaction, authority, and organization not wholly independent upon just when it happened or whether the account is historically accurate.

Lest the search for patterns, for personal and social structures, be understood as a return to formalism, let me hasten to add that a dynamic structuralism also searches for the transformations by which any pattern is being transformed into something else. For example, human growth is something that is neither fixed from the beginning of life nor a random process. Growth occurs as the structure of any one stage is taken up and transformed by the next. Each stage has its own coherence, but is always being transformed into something else. A dynamic structuralism attempts to account for the temporary patterns as well as their transformation. Such a method will be interpreted as neoformalism by some and as neoempiricism by others, for it intentionally draws upon elements of both methods.

The moving patterns of life that are constantly being transformed into new patterns point to a dynamic and ongoing source for all of life. The endless sequence of emerging structural possibilities points to the underlying source that keeps both form and change in relation with each other, each immediately affecting the other. In confessional language the formed but changing source of life is analogous to the creativity of God. In the movement of life from infancy to childhood, to adolescence, to adulthood we experience the creative hand of God who calls us forth by a simple command, "Let us make humanity in our own image..." (Genesis 1:26). The dynamically changing structures of the life cycle reflect the changing regularities of the divine will. God constantly moves toward a new covenant with humanity that deepens and transforms the old without destroying it. In the words of Jesus, "I have not come to destroy the law and the prophets, but to fulfill them" (Matthew 5:18). In the words of Paul, the creation is in travail to bring forth the new (Romans 8:22); or, in the images of Revelation, a new heaven and a new earth shall replace the old (21:1).

Let this not be confused with an optimistic evolutionary view. Our generation knows what the biblical writers knew, that the moving structures from which life is formed are equally capable of destroying life or sustaining it. The dynamic patterns of death are to be found not only in disease, but in the way humanity is polluting the environment, over-populating the globe, unleashing nuclear destruction, and falling into moral decay. We hope and believe that with a better understanding of the structures of destruction, humanity will better be able to limit such structures and nourish life-giving patterns. The hope and trust that constantly spring up in human life are analogous to what we mean confessionally when we speak of faith in God. In faith Christians believe that God's judgment is in the service of love. In the life, death, and resurrection of Jesus Christ we see life in God's will under the judgment of sin. The structures (powers) of death cannot overcome that life, and it springs anew (resurrection) to live as a transforming faith for all who believe. The movement of each person through the various stages of the life cycle allows past patterns to die and be reborn with new possibilities and new hope. Faith in Jesus Christ means that death itself is the occasion of the deepest and most profound of the transformations that characterize all stages of life.

Having described in a brief way the relationship of revelation and the life cycle, let us turn now to an illustration that may make the relationship more vivid. We shall focus upon story-telling because it is so central to the teaching ministry of the church. The stories that we tell one another reflect the trans-formational structures of life. All stories of early childhood, middle childhood, and adolescence have certain patterned fea-tures that deepen and transform what went before. This is undoubtedly also true of the stories that adults tell one another, but for the purposes of this chapter we shall restrict ourselves to the stories of childhood and adolescence.[2]

The stories of preschool children are characterized by a play-ful use of fantasy. The stories may subtly teach certain at-titudes, but those attitudes must be woven into a simply formed and rich use of fantasy. Stories about animals acting as people are delightful. The fairy godmother may come and go, the three little pigs may be eaten and spring alive again, and pooh bear is just as real as Christopher Robin. Reality is elastic and changeable. There is no sharp line between what is thought and what actually happens.[3]

The fantasy stories of early childhood allow children in their imagination to reach far beyond their more immediate circumstances. Such stories express attitudes toward life that are not immediately apparent to the child. Snow White expresses a young girl's fear of growing up; Little Red Ridinghood expresses the reality of "stranger danger." For children these stories are a delightful play of fantasy. They give expression to emotions that the child cannot otherwise name. The stories are told in a setting or ritual intimacy that lets the child feel secure and appreciated. Fantasy stories are touching stories. They allow the child to be in touch with language, emotions, and the storyteller.

The simple story of Jesus' birth, life, death, and resurrection is a story that a preschool child can enjoy as soon as fantasy stories start being told. The fact that Jesus is real and the others only stories makes no difference at all to the preschool child, and the difference can be explained in due time. Of course the telling of the story is most meaningful to a child when the storyteller is in touch with the child, as we explained above. The reference to Jesus' death should neither be eliminated nor dwelt upon. To eliminate references to death at any stage in life is to impoverish it, and this is also true of the preschool years. Stories that make reference to death are the child's way of coping with a very real part of life. The movement to eliminate reference to death was right in objecting to what can become morbid or frightening to children. Better to eliminate than to dwell upon the morbid. However, the movement was wrong is trying to protect children from the reality of death. Death is quite natural and inevitable, and children can be handicapped when all references to it are avoided.

Middle childhood, the time of the elementary school years, brings a remarkable change in a child's abilities. Reality is no longer elastic and fanciful but becomes fixed and tangible. This change is evidenced by many new skills such as reading, telling time, playing games, doing arithmetic, to mention only a few. A child learns how to play by the rules of the game, live by the rules of the classroom, and read by the rules of sentence structure. The world is no longer so fanciful. At least the child learns to separate what he or she is imagining from what is really happening. Children become very concerned about what is fair, and they insist that they get as much as the other children.[4]

The fable is the appropriate story of middle childhood. Fables characteristically have a literal point or a moral to teach. A child of this age quickly understands the point of the fable about the dog that lost its bone in trying to take a bone away from its own reflection in the water. Children can understand the point of the parables or the details of the stories of various persons in the biblical account. However, the child may wonder whether a story really happened or not. The honest answer is the best one, in my judgment. Some things really happened, and some things may not have happened as described, but in both cases God really speaks through the story.

Middle childhood is a literal period. The literalness of this age transforms and deepens the fantasy of the earlier age. Everyone goes through both a period of fantasy and a period of literalness in development toward adulthood. To remain fixed at either level would be to remain immature. At the same time mature faith must have both elements of fantasy and of literalness if it is to reach deeply into our own lives. Christian faith is impoverished without the literal elements within the story of Jesus' birth, life, death, and resurrection. At the same time faith is impoverished without the use of imagination (fantasy) to interpret those events.[5] The line between them is important, but can never be fully established, just as it can never be fully established in the self-interpretation of our own life cycle. Conservative literalism focuses upon the miracles, while liberal literalism focuses upon the moral. Both are important, but neither by itself is sufficient for a fuller understanding of the gospel.

Remarkable new abilities are gained by youth during the time of adolescence.[6] Youth are no longer limited by concrete and literal thinking, nor do they abandon it. Rather the literal is deepened by being able to see causes, anticipate consequences, discover patterns, and consider other possibilities. At the same time youth are prone to play with ideology, jumping from one commitment to another in an effort to find what really fits them. It is a time of high idealism coupled with ideological over-commitment.[7]

The parable is a story especially appropriate to adolescence. The parable is not simply fanciful, nor simply literal, although it contains both elements. Parables are fanciful in that they are "might have been" stories. They may have happened, but the telling may also use fanciful elements. At the same time they undoubtedly refer to comments, events in the hearers experience. First century listeners knew of kings who were defeated without counting the cost before beginning the campaign, or of foolish maidens who came to a wedding without oil for the lamp. The parable contains strong literal possibilities. However, neither the fantasy nor the literalness yields the fullest meaning of a parable.

A parable uses an everyday type event to put a different story-frame on life itself. We understand the parable when we see the relationship between the story-frame of the parable and the story-frame of our own lives. This requires an analogical use of reason. Neither fanciful nor literal elements exhaust the meaning of a parable, even though both are present. The hearer who understands the way in which the good Samaritan acted will find himself or herself in a different story-frame. The hearer who understands the story of the prodigal son will find his or her own prodigality set in a different frame. Youth are able to reason in this way and are at the point of searching out the frame of their own future life stories.

We might well explore out how the life commitments of early adulthood, the responsibilities of middle adulthood, and the search for integrity during later adulthood, each in its own way, and all in their relatedness, become ways by which we may understand God's powerful guiding presence. However, such an effort would go beyond the present limits. Let it suffice to say that in the stories we tell to children and youth we glimpse the transformational structures that reflect the way in which God's will comes ever anew to humankind as a transforming and saving possibility.

Notes

1. For a brief but difficult introduction to structuralism, see Jean Piaget, *Structuralism,* Basic Books, 1970.
2. Eric Auerbach, *Mimesis, The Representation of Reality in Western Literature,* Doubleday, 1957.
3. Jean Piaget, *Six Psychological Studies,* Vintage Books, 1968; Sigmund Freud, "Formulations Regarding Two Principles of Mental Functioning," in *A General Selection from the Works of Sigmund Freud,* ed. John Rickman, Doubleday, 1957.
4. Jean Piaget, *The Moral Judgment of the Child,* Free Press, 1965.
5. H. Richard Niebuhr, *The Meaning of Revelation,* Macmillan, 1960.
6. Bärbel Inhelder and Jean Piaget, *The Growth of Logical Thinking from Childhood to Adolescence,* Basic Books, 1958.
7. Erik Erikson, *Identity, Youth and Crisis,* W. W. Norton, 1968.

PART IV

RANDOLPH CRUMP MILLER

CHAPTER 14

EXEMPLAR OF PROCESS AND RELATIONSHIP

Boardman W. Kathan

For over a quarter of a century Randolph Crump Miller has exerted a profound influence on the shaping of religion and education in the United States, Canada and many other countries around the world. It could be said that, just as George Albert Coe was the giant of the religious education movement in the first half of this century, Miller has occupied that position so far in the second half. For evidence, one need only consider: the eighteen books, (several translated into Japanese and Korean) and scores of articles he has written; the countless sermons, lectures, and workshops he has given in this country and throughout the world; the thousands of students he has taught and counseled; the new curriculum he helped develop and write; and the prestigious journal he has edited for twenty years.

Undergirding everything that he has done is his unwavering commitment to communicate the Judeo-Christian faith in a way that would be relevant and helpful to a scientifically sophisticated, skeptical, and cynical age. Primarily a theologian, he has always explored the educational implications of the truth-of-God-in-relation-to-humankind. Professionally an educator, he has always used the theological and philosophical tools of his craft. As a theologian of process and relationship, he has been and continues to be an outstanding exemplar of both.

Randolph Crump Miller was born October 1, 1910 in Fresno, California, the son of Ray Oakley Miller and Laura Belle Crump Miller. His father was born on a West Virginia farm and became a minister of the Christian Church (Disciples of Christ) after graduation from Bethany College and Yale Divinity School. His mother came from near Pittsburgh, Pennsylvania, the daughter of a coal mine owner. After serving churches in Fort Wayne, Indiana, and Fresno, California, his father became an Episcopalian and was the pastor of St. James Church in Los Angeles for nearly thirty years. Ray Oakley Miller received an honorary doctorate of divinity from Bethany.

In a brief autobiographical sketch in *This We Can Believe,* Randy has written: "My father's religious outlook was a major influence. He was an intelligent, liberal, Episcopal clergyman."[1] His father was always a liberal in the sense of being open-minded. Ray Oakley Miller had written a book in 1917 entitled, *Modernist Studies in the Life of Jesus.* Although the word, "modernist," was a fighting word at that time, the elder Miller defined it as "a use of natural and scientific tests in religious thinking," but "not without a genuine sympathy for and an appreciation and appropriation of the fundamental elements of idealism and faith."[2] The volume concluded with a statement of his liberal faith:

> A liberal is one whose blood is growing warmer, whose charity is growing broader, whose vision is growing clearer, who in the last analysis, is deeply in love with life.[3]

In many ways Randy has exemplified the spirit of his father, and their relationship was a major factor in his life.

In the same autobiographical sketch, he wrote:

> My father's parish provided an atmosphere in which we were free to seek new ideas and fresh ways of thinking. Against such a background, I was free to ask questions, and when I discovered that my father as a committed Christian was open to the reformulation and even the discarding of certain beliefs and was aware of scientific advances and the political implications of Christian living, it was easy for me to begin thinking on my own.[4]

Randy has described his mother as a healthy, outgoing, athletic person, who taught his father how to drive. It came as a great blow when his mother suddenly became ill with multiple sclerosis and was confined to a wheelchair for the last twelve years of her life. Randy was in college when the illness first struck and it caused him to struggle with the problems of good and evil and the nature of God as all-powerful and all good. How could a good God allow this to happen? He has put it this way:

> In my course with Professor Robert Denison, I was exposed to the thinking of William James, John Dewey, and Henry Nelson Wieman, among others. It was James who spoke directly to my problem. I began to see the universe pretty much as he did, as a pluralistic process of interrelationships, in which God is at work but not in complete control. If I could take seriously the fact that God has an environment, is limited in power, faces opposing forces, and works against evil that is also real, I could find a place for a God of love in the face of my mother's illness.[5]

In the preface to *Be Not Anxious*, he wrote: "Surely I learned from a mother who suffered from multiple sclerosis for almost twenty years and whose faith sustained her and kept her free from anxiety." For Randy and even more for his younger brother and sister, their mother's illness was the focal point of their development as children.

Randy attended Harvard Military School, enjoyed church school and church, sang in the junior choir, and served as crucifer for the senior choir. He first felt a call to the ministry, not in some mystical or supernatural way, but in a response to a dull sermon preached by a minister in a little church in Ben Lomond the summer after finishing high school. Randy never doubted what his vocation was, but he has often been suspicious of his fitness for it. This "conversion" experience built upon the background of his previous life, but the chief influences were his parents.

His undergraduate work was done at Pomona College. There he was introduced to philosophy by Robert Denison, whose courses were thorough and comprehensive. "But again it was the *man* who made all the difference, and I loved Robert Denison. I worked for him and so I learned more than anyone else."[6]

After graduation from Pomona College in 1931, Randy did graduate study at Yale, where the philosophy that began at Pomona was developed further. The influence of William James remained strong in his thinking, but his religious and

intellectual needs began to be met by the empirical theology of
Douglas Clyde Macintosh. He took courses in psychology of
religion under Luther Weigle and Hugh Hartshorne; he was
thrilled with Robert Calhoun's course on the history of Christian doctrine; he took every course offered by Macintosh.
Randy wrote his doctoral dissertation on Wieman and the
Chicago school of process thought while he was a special student at the Episcopal Theological School in Cambridge, Mas-
sachusetts in 1935–36, and received his Ph.D. from Yale in
1936. He wrote later in his life:

> I think the major directions of my thinking were pretty well estab-
> lished by 1936. The influence of such men as my father, Denison,
> and Macintosh were strongest, among those whom I knew person-
> ally; and my reading of Wieman, James, and a few others rounded
> out my philosophy of religion. I was obviously an empiricist and a
> liberal, and I liked both labels and still do. There were new influ-
> ences and new interests during the next sixteen years, but I doubt if
> they altered the direction of my thought as it was established when I
> thought through my mother's illness back in 1929.[7]

While at Cambridge he received an invitation to teach at the
Church Divinity School of the Pacific—for room and board! He
had thought of the parish ministry as his real vocation, and
teaching in a seminary had never occurred to him, yet he accepted it immediately. The direction of his professional career
was established. At Berkeley he taught Christian ethics and
philosophy of religion, and became chaplain to Episcopalian
students at the University of California. He was ordained an
Episcopal priest on January 6, 1937.

It was not until 1940 that Miller was asked to teach his first
course in Christian education. He had never taken any classes
on the subject and would have preferred to teach theology: "I
never understood why I was not allowed to teach theology,
except that I was considered dangerous." He credits his wife,
Muriel, whom he had married on June 9, 1938, for sharing her
notes from a course she had taken on the subject at Berkeley
Baptist Divinity School. 1940 became a turning point for a
"frustrated theologian" turned religious educator. It was also in
1940 that he finished his work as Episcopal chaplain and became vicar of St. Alban's Parish, a small store-front church in

Albany, California, which he built up from a small, dedicated core of members to a congregation of over two hundred fifty. Miller continued on the seminary faculty until 1952. During those years he also became chairman of the department of Christian education of the Diocese of California and a member of the curriculum division of the National Council of the Protestant Episcopal Church. He also chaired the Hazen Pacific Coast Theology Group.

In 1951 he was invited to join the faculty of the Divinity School of Yale University in the field of religious education. This presented a dilemma since Randy's preference was in the area of theology and philosophy. As he looked back over the previous decade, however, he could see that he was in great demand as a Christian educator and in no demand as a theologian. He was giving lectures coast to coast in Christian education. His 1943 volume, *Guide for Church School Teachers,* was in a second edition, and *The Clue to Christian Education,* was outselling his theological book for lay people, *Religion Makes Sense,* two to one. Professor Paul Vieth and Dean Liston Pope made it clear that they wanted a person trained as he was, and that they wanted him to make theology relevant in courses in education. He was not to teach gadgets or how to fix a movie machine. As he wrote:

> Chiefly I had to decide whether I ought to spend my full time in Christian education, and this I was not sure of. I would rather teach theology (and this is still true), but it looked as if everything was pushing me in the direction of Christian education.[8]

Thus he went to Yale, and at the age of forty-one embarked on a new career in an nondenominational seminary.

Until 1963 Randy was professor on the Luther A. Weigle Fund. It was during these productive years that he taught as a colleague of Dr. Paul Vieth, developed a comprehensive list of course offerings in Christian education, worked with both B.D. and Ph.D. students, and had eight books published. He served as director of Christian education at St. Paul's Episcopal Parish in New Haven and later at Trinity Church on the Green. He completed his work as a consultant and author for the Seabury Series of the Episcopal Church, and became active in the professors' and other sections of the Division of Christian Education of the National Council of Churches. For three years he served as Chairman of the board of directors of the multi-faith Religious Education Association and in 1958 became editor of its journal, *Religious Education*. On his first sabbatical from Yale in 1959–60 he and his wife studied at the Ecumenical Institute in Switzerland and visited many centers in Europe. He also wrote a book, *Christian Nurture and the Church*, and a study guide for the World Council of Christian Education.

After Professor Vieth's retirement in 1963, Miller became Horace Bushnell professor of Christian nurture at Yale. From 1965 to 1972 Dr. Iris V. Cully was associate professor of religious education, the first woman in the history of Yale Divinity School with faculty rank. Randy's sabbatical trip to the Far East, Middle East, and teaching in India and Lebanon in 1966–67 led to the book, *The Language Gap and God*. A third sabbatical trip in 1970 under the auspices of the World Council of Christian Education, took him and his wife to New Zealand, Australia, Indonesia, and Southeast Asia. These trips overseas have greatly enriched his teaching and writing and have provided many opportunities for lecturing and speaking to educators from many countries. Through the years he has also been a visiting professor at Harvard, Episcopal Theological School, Union, Berkeley, Serampore (India), United Theological College (British Columbia), and other institutions. Randy has received the honorary D.D. degree from Pacific School of Religion and Episcopal Divinity School, and the doctorate of sacred theology from Church Divinity School of the Pacific.

Randolph Crump Miller is, first of all, a man, a "complete" human being. To know him is to encounter a well-organized, integrated personality, who is in control of himself, has seemingly complete self-confidence, and knows what he believes and where he stands. He loves people, enjoys parties and dinners, and is always ready to engage in sparkling conversation. Since high school days he has been a spectator-sports enthusiast, primarily for baseball, football, and auto-racing. When he lived in California, before the major league teams discovered the West Coast, he managed somehow to squeeze in a baseball game or two on his occasional trips East. One of the pleasures of living in New Haven has been the proximity to New York, and it was sheer delight when the New York Giants had to play home games in the Yale Bowl for several seasons! For twenty Sundays of the year, and Monday evenings too, the TV in the Miller household is abuzz with pro football. A special antenna had to be secured so that the New York channels could be picked up. A particular joy as a father was watching his son, Frank, play quarterback for Hopkins Grammar School, as well as accompanying him to major league baseball games. For one period of his life, Miller owned a Jaguar and a racy cap to match it, and he recounts with relish driving it over 100 m.p.h. on a straight stretch of British highway. One of the highlights of a semester sabbatical in California was watching the first Grand Prix through the streets of Long Beach. One sport he still participates in is swimming. Tennis he gave up quite early when his appendix started to act up.

Miller has one of the finest collections of jazz records, including a first recording of a Scott Joplin piano rag. He has lectured in many places on "theology and jazz" and has kept up with each new development in the field. The first "jazz vespers" done by the Singleton Palmer band in St. Louis in 1961 was a singular experience of pleasure for him. Examples of various jazz or folk masses are also included in his lectures. He is a connoisseur of fine coffee and can extol at great length the merits of various brands, whether Turkish, Irish, or other, and he grinds and blends his own. The experience of being a guest overnight at the Millers is capped by having one of his own special brews served to you in bed in the morning! Randy also knows and enjoys pipe tobacco and boasts a magnificent collection of pipes for all occasions. He enjoys playing bridge, going to concerts and plays, and dancing, but, most of all, his family and friends.

To know Miller is to know him as a devoted husband and loving father (and grandfather). He has written: "A great deal of life's richest meanings have come from my experiences as a family man."[9] One who is privileged to read the letters to his children from 1936–1970, is impressed by the richness of his nuclear family life and the close relationships of the extended families to which he belongs. He had met his first wife, Muriel

Hallett, at the beginning of his student work in Berkeley in 1936 when she was a senior at the University of California. As a student at St. Margaret's House the following year, she took one of Miller's courses. She used to say that he would take her on a date and quiz her about the course. Randy wrote later: "If she didn't get something, there was something wrong with my teaching. She was a wonderful student, for she always did all the reading and got her papers in on time."[10] They were married on June 9, 1938 and took a honeymoon trip across the country by car. Their ten years of marriage were busy ones, with many activities in seminary and parish, much entertaining, and especially the addition of four daughters, Barbara, Phyllis, Carol and Muriel. Miller mentions the death of his wife in the preface to *Religion Makes Sense:*

> On May 13, 1948, my wife died suddenly from poliomyelitis, leaving me with four young daughters and a legacy of love and warmth and help which defies description. Muriel Hallett Miller was for ten brief years the chief source of my inspiration and creative ability. Her outgoing personality permeated every aspect of our home and work and play together.[11]

Miller was blessed with a marvelous mother-in-law who helped care for the children and keep the household organized. As he said in 1952: "For the next two years, Mrs. Hallett ran my house and took care of my children. She was wonderful, and I learned to love her even more. These were hard years, though, although my work did not seem to suffer."[12]

In a brief autobiographical reference, Miller describes the next event which might be called providential:

> I was in Virginia for some lectures, due to a chance invitation after others had refused. While there, also by chance, I met a young widow. Our meeting was so brief that normally no one would notice it. Yet both of us saw the significance of that occasion. There was some kind of disclosure to which we both responded. Call it chance, call it intuition, call it love. Within a year we were married.[13]

On June 16, 1950, Miller and Elizabeth Fowlkes were wed in Richmond, Virginia. Elizabeth had a son, Frank, and a daughter, Rives, from her first marriage. Thus "Randy" and "Lib" suddenly had a combined family of six. Their years as a growing, happy family are full of stories of schools and church, neighbors and friends, clubs and socials, orchestra and practice, trips and vacations, sports and cars, dates and weddings. Can you imagine having six teenagers in the family all at the same time? Now the same steadfast love and support is extended to the growing number of grandchildren. Randy concluded his volume of letters with these words:

> I think that these have been wonderful years for all of us and as I re-read what I have written I realize anew what a fortunate person I have been in both my wife and my children. I look back to that picture of the whole tribe (Abraham and his children?) taken when Muriel and Jim were married. It is already outdated by new arrivals, but it tells a wonderful story. Our children, their spouses, and our grandchildren have done us proud, and we are proud. And we love you all."[14]

Randolph Miller is preeminently a theologian. The mention of a theologian still evokes an image of an armchair quarterback who second-guesses God from the safe confines of the grandstand rather than risking being dumped on the stadium turf. Not so Miller. He has been too warm and outgoing a personality and too much a family man and pastor to be removed or cloistered from the pain and hurt, the conflict and compromises of daily life. Randy's theology has been shaped and tested by his studies and by his personal and pastoral experiences. Theological fads have come and gone in the past forty-five years, but Miller has grown and developed as a process theologian par excellence. He has written:

> Process thinking provides a metaphysical framework for all of our thinking. It gives us a view of the cosmos that accounts for the working of God, for the development of novelty, chance, and freedom, for the experiences of suffering and evil as well as those of transformation and joy, for the meaning of living in community and for the validity of being an individual, for understanding that all existence is a matter of becoming and perishing in the context of a continuity underwritten by God, for grasping the meaning of the past and the present as they point to an open future—open even to God himself.[15]

In his book, *The American Spirit in Theology*, Miller has traced the development of process theology, which he calls a distinctive American contribution. The significant elements of this approach are radical empiricism, pragmatism, and pluralism, building upon the insights of William James, John Dewey, and Alfred North Whitehead. In an article in *The Christian Century*, he wrote:

> With the coming of World War II there was a Barthian blackout of this kind of thinking. The emphasis was on revelation and the wholly other God. Barthian ways of thinking predominated. Slowly the whole of theology was permeated by what was called neo-orthodoxy. Most of the churches held to a standard biblical orthodoxy....[16]

John A. T. Robinson's *Honest to God* and the "death-of-God movement" were reactions to the biblical literalism or supernaturalism, not to the empirically based process theology of Wieman. Miller is obviously pleased that times have changed, that there is a new readiness to consider process modes of thought, and that other theologians, Protestant and Catholic, have adopted the process model. He has also pointed out recently that this approach can be very helpful in meeting the problems of racism, sexism, and the third world, since process theology is not a culture-bound or closed system. Randy has been called a theologian of both process and relationship, and he was indebted to Martin Buber and Reuel Howe, among others, for their contributions to his thought. In his recent book he wrote:

> Because of the significance of relationships between people as a means of reaching spiritual health, because of the evidence that the effectiveness of teachers is in terms of their contagious faith, because of the "I-Thou" emphasis in the achieving of community, we begin to understand how God's grace works through human channels. The love, forgiveness, and the redemptive and transforming power of God reaches persons chiefly through other persons.[17]

Randy would add that this happens primarily through the family, and of this he has had first-hand experience.

In the letter to the Ephesians it is written: "And his gifts were that some should be apostles, some prophets, some evangelists, some pastors and teachers..." (4:11, RSV). Randy has been both a pastor and teacher through most of his professional career. His teaching has been filled with concern for the personal growth of his students; his pastoral work has been enriched by educational interests. Never content to labor only in the groves of academe, he has given his time and talent to local parishes as priest, counselor, or director of Christian education. In his person he has tried to bridge the perennial gap between seminary and church, between clergy and laity, pulpit and pew. This commitment to the local church has always impressed students who wondered whether there was any practical application to the philosophy and theology discussed in the classroom. It was reassuring to know that the theories had been field-tested, and that the professor himself was on the "front-line" of the skirmish. Some of his books grew out of the attempt to make the historic faith speak to the problems of lay people; several consisted of sermons preached in a local church.

Even his books in Christian education have grown out of many workshops and institutes with volunteer church school teachers as well as trained clergy and directors, and in manuscript form they were studied in class. For a seminary student and young pastor during those years there was a sense of excitement as we shared in the development of these books at Yale Divinity School and as we sought to put them to work in local parishes. There was also the frustration of counseling untrained teachers who wanted a step-by-step lesson for next Sunday morning and not a theological understanding of God! Miller shared these concerns and appreciated the small gains and victories we reported in family worship, preparation for baptism or confirmation, adult education, and parent-youth dialogue. As both pastor and teacher, it was the spirit and personality of the person that was communicated, and his faith was contagious.

One way of looking at his prolific career as an author and editor is to divide it into three periods. The first period covered the decade from 1940 to 1950 is characterized by a generalist approach to religion, reflecting ethical, pastoral, and educational concerns. His first book, *What We Can Believe* in 1941 is "addressed to the modern man who wants to know what Chris-

tianity has to offer him during these days of tragedy and crisis."
His second book, *A Guide for Church School Teachers*, grew out of
a series of lectures he was asked to give at leadership institutes
in parishes in Berkeley and San Francisco. It was in his third
volume, *Christianity and the Contemporary Scene,* coedited by
Henry H. Shires, that he laid down the challenge he has re-
sponded to ever since: "A theology for Christian education is
needed. The objectives, theory and methods of Christian education need to be undergirded and perhaps altered by a more
self-conscious theological reconstruction."[18] Randy's *A Clue to
Christian Education* was the beginning of an answer and was the
first of a trilogy of books on the subject published by Charles
Scribner's. Three other books, *A Symphony of the Christian Year,
Religion Makes Sense,* and *Be Not Anxious,* were also developed in
this first period and included reworked sermons and medita-
tions preached at St. Alban's Church or elsewhere.

The second period of writing, 1952–1965, is characterized by
a more specialized, systematic attention to Christian education,
roughly coinciding with Miller's first period at Yale Divinity
School. In *The Clue to Christian Education* he had tried "to work
out the relevance of Christian theology in terms of the relationship experienced by various age groups." In the second book of
the trilogy, *Biblical Theology and Christian Education,* he looked at
the biblical record of the mighty acts of God as the source of
theology: "Of course, all Christian theology is based on the
Bible, but I have been concerned that the Bible itself illuminate
the relationships of daily living in terms of the resources of the
gospel."[19] In *Christian Nurture and the Church,* Randy explored
the significance of the nature of the church for Christian education. His basic thesis was that genuine Christian education
takes place within a Christian community. The church provides
an environment for real encounter between persons which
gives meaning to key concepts of Christian living like faith,
love, hope and grace. During these years a textbook, *Education
for Christian Living,* was written to serve as a guide course in
religious education in colleges and seminaries. *Your Children's
Religion* appeared during this period as a guide for parents and
Youth Considers Parents as People, was written for young people to
help them understand the needs and developmental stages of

their elders. A smaller book, *I Remember Jesus,* is an attempt to present an eye-witness account of the ministry of Jesus through the eyes of a boy of the time who in later life recalls the story. The mid-1960s marked the beginning of his third period, continuing to the present time. It can be characterized as a period of return to some philosophical themes of the first period on a more mature and sophisticated level. We see here the fruits of a lifetime of work and experience. It is no surprise that in these years there should appear a complete revision of *Be Not Anxious* under the title, *Living with Anxiety,* or that he should choose the subject of death for full treatment in *Live Until You Die,* or that, after exploring the language of relationships in many ways, he should examine the language of words in the book, *The Language Gap and God.* In this period he has produced *The American Spirit in Theology,* a book which had been "in process" ever since his college philosophy course and his doctoral dissertation. He has also issued a rewriting of his very first book under the title, *This We Can Believe.*

Worthy of special mention is his work with the development of the Seabury Series by the Episcopal Church. Miller had written curriculum material for the Cloister Series, *The Challenge of the Church,* and had revised the course, *Climbers of the Steep Ascent,* but the revolutionary new approach of the Seabury Series captured his imagination and stirred his rhetorical juices. It is not generally known that the admirable resource book, *More Than Words,* was revised by him before publication. Of great importance, also, is his unprecedented long tenure as editor of *Religious Education,* read by Protestant, Catholic, and Jewish subscribers in forty countries. Billed as "a platform for the free discussion of religious issues and their bearing on education," the journal was a springboard for Miller into the bewildering issues and movements of the last twenty years. The journal during this period was shaped by an extraordinary theologian-educator, who sought to relate theory and practice and to shape the future of religion and education. At conferences and conventions he was constantly on the lookout for papers and presentations that would address these issues in a sound, and scholarly, yet understandable, way. His frustration was the lack of adequate space to include much material that met his high standards of quality and value. He also has served since 1976 as a member of the editorial board of *The New Review of Books and Religion*.

How can one appraise the abundant life and productive work of such a person still in mid-stream? His effort to construct an adequate theological foundation for educational ministry broke new ground for a generation of educators, which included Lewis J. Sherrill, James D. Smart, Iris V. Cully, Gerard Sloyan, David R. Hunter, D. Campbell Wyckoff, Eugene Borowitz, Gabriel Moran, and many others. He directed doctoral studies of several persons who are now leaders in religious education thought and practice, including Sara Little, Neely Dixon McCarter, Will Kennedy, Charles Melchert, Lloyd Sheneman, and David Steward. His vision of educational ministry has broadened the horizons of pastors and teachers to encompass not only home and church, school and synagogue, college and university, but the problems of language games and linguistic analysis, preparation for death and dying, and trends in theology and morality. For over forty years he has been on the growing edge of religion and education and a chief architect of its theory and practice. His writings and lectures have reached an international audience, where he is a respected and admired leader. However, through it all shines a personality who gives substance, meaning, and value to all the words through relationships of love, caring, and support. Miller has written:

> It is in the nature of God, as conceived by process thought, to bring things together, to work for harmony, and to restore relationship. If, then, we can experience God's presence as interpreted by process thought, we can be reconciled to each other and to God.[20]

In honor of a theologian who is also an avid baseball fan, let us conclude with a favorite quotation from Henry Nelson Wieman:

> But if you want to find out the true spirit of baseball in all the glory of a passion you must not go to the big leagues. You must go to the backyard, the sand-lot, the side street, and the school ground. There it is not a profession, it is a passion. When a passion becomes a profession, it often ceases to be a passion. That is as true of religion as it is of baseball. Among the professionals you find a

superb mastery and a great technique, but not too frequently the pure devotion. Perhaps in baseball the passion is not too important, but in religion it is all important. A religion that is not passionate simply is not worth considering. Therefore, I say, we need more sand-lot religion."[21]

Notes

1. R. C. Miller, *This We Can Believe*, Hawthorn Books, 1976.
2. Ray Oakley Miller, *Modernist Studies in the Life of Jesus*, Sherman, French & Co., 1917.
3. Ibid.
4. R. C. Miller, op cit.
5. R. C. Miller, op cit.
6. R. C. Miller, from autobiographical sketch, 1951. Unpublished *Letters to Our Children*, 1936-70.
7. Ibid., p. 72.
8. Ibid., p. 98.
9. Ibid., p. 73.
10. Ibid., p. 10.
11. R. C. Miller, *Religion Makes Sense*, The Seabury Press, 1950, p. ii.
12. R. C. Miller, Unpublished *Letters to Our Children*, 1936-70, p. 73.
13. R. C. Miller, *This We Can Believe*.
14. R. C. Miller, Unpublished *Letters to Our Children*, 1936-70, p. 161.
15. R. C. Miller, "Process Thinking and Religious Education," *Anglican Theological Review*, July, 1975, p. 271.
16. R. C. Miller, "Empiricism and Process Theology: God Is What God Does," *The Christian Century*, March 24, 1976, p. 284.
17. R. C. Miller, *This We Can Believe*.
18. R. C. Miller and Henry H. Shires, editors, *Christianity and the Contemporary Scene*, Morehouse-Gorham Co., 1943, p. 198.
19. R. C. Miller, *Biblical Theology and Christian Education*, Charles Scribner's Sons, p. vii.
20. R. C. Miller, "Process Thinking and Religious Education," p. 284.
21. R. C. Miller, *The American Spirit in Theology*, United Church Press, 1974, p. 92.

BIBLIOGRAPHY:
THE WORKS OF
RANDOLPH CRUMP MILLER

ARTICLES IN MAGAZINES AND JOURNALS

1935

"The Church's Social Dilemmas."*The Churchman* Vol. CXLIX, Number 23, December 1, 1935, 14.

1936

"Liberal Religious Thought Today: Professor Wieman's Position." *The Churchman*, April 15, 1936, 14–15.

"Liberalism: Method or Creed?" *The Churchman*, June 15, 1936, 16–31.

"Has Liberalism a Theology?" *The Churchman*, September 15, 1936, 15–16.

1937

"O, Principle of Concretion!" *The Chronicle*, January 1937, 89–90.

"Seminaries and the Curriculum." *The Southern Churchman*, July 3, 1937, 5–6.

"Theologs and Clinics." *The Churchman*, March 15, 1937, 17.

"Religious Realism in America." *The Modern Churchman*, December 1937, 495–506.

1938

"What the Young Cleric Studies." *The Los Angeles Churchman*, January 1938, 4–5.

1939

"Is Temple a Realist?" *Journal of Religion*, January 1939, 44–54.

"The Western Church Grows Up," *Los Angeles Churchman*, May 1939, 3,6,8.

"The Importance of Our Divinity Schools." *The Chronicle*, July 1939, 232–34.

"Adventure of Faith." *The Southern Churchman*, September 16, 1939, 56,8.

"What Is Christianity?" *The Churchman*, Dec. 15, 1939, 14–15.

1940

"The New Naturalism and Christianity." *Anglican Theological Review*, January 1940, 25–35.

"God in a World at War." *The Churchman*, February 15, 1940, 15–16.

"Theology in Transition," *Journal of Religion,* April 1940, 160-168.
"Empiricism and Analogical Theology." *Christendom,* Summer 1940, 399-411.
"The New Testament and Church Unity." *The Churchman,* July 1940, 12-13.
"Professor Macintosh and Empirical Theology." *The Personalist,* Winter 1940, 1949.

1941

"Is Temple a Realist?" *The Chronicle,* (Poughkeepsie, New York) February 1941, 101-104.
"Why I Don't Go to Church." *The Churchman,* March 1, 1941, 13-14.
"What the Seminaries Are Trying to Do." *Los Angeles Churchman,* March 1941.
"Decently and in Order." *The Pacific Churchman,* June 1941, 15-17.
"Religion in the Home." *The Witness,* November 13, 1941, 4-6.

1942

"Beware of Spiritual Sabotage." *The Churchman,* March 15, 1942, 12-13.
"Streamlining the Church." *The Churchman,* February 1, 1942, 10.
"Easter and Prayer," *Pacific Churchman* April 1942.
"From Drake's Bay On. . . ." *The Living Church,* October 4, 1942, 12-15.
"Prayer in Wartime." *The Christian Century,* November 25, 1942, 1456-1457.

1943

"Lessons That Children Like." *The Churchman,* January 1, 1943, 9-10.
"Liberalism is not Dead." *The Witness,* January 28, 1943, 11-12.
"Secondary Schools in Christian Education." *The Churchman,* August 1, 1943, 6-7.'

1944

"Old Themes in New Dress." *The Living Church,* February 13, 1944, 11-12.
"The Quiz Kids Invade School of California Parish." *The Witness,* October 19, 1944, 5-6.
"Interdenominational Education." *The Living Church,* October 22, 1944, 16-17.

1945

"Empirical Method and Its Critics." *Anglican Theological Review,* January 1945, 27-34.
"Is It True What They Say about Henry?" *The Chronicle* January 1945, 79-80.
"Overcoming Our Troubles." *The Pulpit,* April 1945, 88-90.
"The Relevance of Christian Ethics." *Religion in Life,* Spring 1945, 205-15.
"Prayer Book Christianity," *The Chronicle,* April 1945, 152-53.
"The Church School of Tomorrow." *The Southern Churchman,* September 1, 1945, 3-4.

"Why Man Works." *The Witness,* October 11, 1945, 11-12.
"The Prayer Book and the Red Network." *The Churchman,* November 15, 1945, 12.
"The King's Highway," *Chronicle,* Dec. 1945, 57-59.

1946

"Freedom and Jazz." *The Witness,* January 24, 1946, 11-12.
"Medicine and Religion." *Pacific Churchman,* January 1946, 24-28.
"Education in the Episcopal Church." *The Churchman,* May 15, 1946, 9.
"Vocational Giver." *The Living Church,* June 16, 1946.
"Liberal Evangelical Theology." *The Witness,* June 17, 1946, 11-12.
"Bobby Sox Religion." *Religious Education,* March-April, 1946, 107-13.
"Weaknesses and Resources of the Christian Church." *Journal of Religious Thought,* Autumn-Winter 1946, 16-33.
"God as Idea and as Living." *Christendom,* Winter 1946, 57-64.

1947

"God in the Atomic Age." *The Chronicle* (Poughkeepsie, New York) February 1947, 89-91.
"Where Our Creeds Came From." *Pacific Churchman,* March 1947, 5-7.

1948

"Our Common Biblical Heritage." *The Witness,* November 25, 1948, 12-14.
"A Barber's Dream." *Forth,* March 1948.
"Education for Living." *The Southern Churchman,* October 16, 1948, 3-4.
"Toward a New Curriculum." *The Living Church,* November 7, 1948, 13-14.

1949

"Things Are Happening at the Pacific," *Witness,* January 20, 1949, 5-6.
"New Church School Curriculum to Offer Fine Material." *The Witness,* March 31, 1949, 3-18.
"When Life Seems Hard." *The Southern Churchman,* March 5, 1949, 3-4.
"New Curriculum Under Way." *The Churchman,* May 15, 1949.
"Dialogue Sermons for Radio." *Southern Churchman,* July 1949, 5-6, 8.
"Shakespeare of the Prayerbook." *The Southern Churchman,* August 13, 1949, 3-4.
"The Old Man and Liturgicum." *The Witness,* September 1, 1949, 15-17.
"Christian Education Report." *Southern Churchman,* September 10, 1949, 7-8.
"A Barber's Dream." *The Southern Churchman,* October 29, 1949.
"California's Bishops." *The Living Church,* October 2, 1949, 20-24.

1950

"Gadgets and the Kingdom of God." *The Living Church,* June 4, 1950, 12-13.
"Through Light and Dark the Road Leads On." *The Southern Churchman,* October 7, 1950, 6-8.
"Subversiveness of the Bill of Rights." *The Witness,* December 7, 1950, 10-12.

1951

"Gremlins and Christianity." *The Churchman,* February 1, 1951, 13-14.
"Brothers of the Faith." *The Witness,* March 1, 1951, 14-16.
"Food for the Spirit." *The Churchman,* April 15, 1951, 10.
"Catholics and Education." *The Churchman,* May 15, 1951, 11-12.
"God and the Nations." *The Churchman,* July 1951, 7-9.
"Peter, Patmos and Peace." *The Witness,* September 20, 1951, 11-13.
"The Mind of Christ." *Southern Churchman,* September 23, 1951, 6-7.
"Where are America's Moral Standards?" *The Living Church,* September 23, 1951, 16-17.
"Pastoral Psychology and Christian Education." *Pastoral Psychology,* October 1951.
"You Too Can Be A Teacher." *The Churchman,* November 1, 1951, 11-12.
"The Protestant Episcopal Church is Catholic." *The Witness,* November 29, 1951, 7-9.
"The Holy Catholic Church is Protestant." *The Witness,* December 6, 1951, 10-12.

1952

"Authority, Scripture and Tradition." *Religion in Life,* Autumn 1952, 551-52.
"Theology and the Understanding of Children." *Pastoral Psychology,* June 1952, 1-2.
"Women in the Church." *The Witness,* July 10, 1952, 9-11.
"Christian Education as a Theological Discipline and Method." *Yale Divinity News,* November 1952, 1-2.

1953

"Three Ministerial Attitudes." *The Witness,* January 1953, 9-11.
"Ministry a Partnership." *The Messenger,* June 16, 1953, 12-15.
"Congressional Investigation of the Prophets." *The Churchman,* May 15, 1953, 8-9.
"Books Children Own." *The Churchman,* April 1, 1953, 10-11.
"Christian Education as a Theological Discipline and Method." *Religious Education,* November-December 1953.

1954

"Children and Death." *Church School Worker,* February 1954, 49-51.
"Human Relations and Christian Education." *World Christian Education,* First Quarter 1954, 3-5.
"Teaching to Create Faith." *The Baptist Reader,* October 1954, 5, 16.
"Americanism, Communism and Fascism." *The Witness,* September 1954, 11-13.
"The New Lessons." *The Witness,* November 25, 1954, 12-13.

1955

"The Seabury Series Launched." *The Witness,* May 15, 1955, 3-4.
"Something New in Religous Education." *The Churchman,* May ? 1955.
"The Family Worships Together." *Presbyterian Survey,* August 1955, 16-17.

"The Family Service." *The Living Church,* August 7, 1955, 22-23.
"Family Worship in the Church." *The Witness,* November 20, 1955, 9-11.

1956

"Family Worship in the Church." *Church School Worker,* January 1956, 55-58.
"Education for Redemption." *International Journal of Religious Education,* March 1956, 12-13.
"Should I Make My Child go to Church School?" *The International Journal of Religious Education,* September 1956, 4-5.
"The Education of Christians." *The Pulpit,* May 1956, 6-7.
"The Demand is Answered." *Episcopal Church News,* October 14, 1956, 25-41.

1957

"Revelation, Relevance, and Relationships." *Religion in Life,* Winter 1957-58, 132-433.
"Ambassadors for Christ." *The Pulpit Digest,* February 1957, 27-30.
"How Shall a Christian Deal with Conscience and Compromise?" *Earnest Worker,* November 1957, 20-21.
"Anxiety in Christian Education." *The Pulpit,* April 1957, 4-5.
"The Family Worships Together." *The Baptist Leader,* September 1957, 5-6, 16.

1958

"Sunday Morning Worship Family Style. *"Presbyterian Action,* August 1958, 14-15.
"The Abundant Life." *The Churchman,* December 1958.
"Probleme der Christlichen Unterweisung in den Vereinigten Staaten." *Lutherische Rundschau,* August 1958, 138-51.
"Christian Education in the United States." *Lutheran World,* September 1958.
"Christian Faith and Life Series." *Union Seminary Quarterly Review,* November 1958, 37-46.

1959

"The Church's Nurture in Christian Education." *The Christian Educator,* January-March 1959, 7-9.
"The Big Family Can Be Redemptive." *International Journal of Religious Education,* April 1959, 6-7.
"The God of the Bible." *Children's Religion,* June 1959, 6-8.
"Redemption in the Family." *International Journal of Religious Education,* December 1959, 13,48.
"Theology and Religious Education." *Religion in Education,* Spring 1959, 73-75.

1960

"The Bible Answers Our Needs," *Pulpit Digest,* February 1960, 37-40.
"Religious Education in Europe." *Religious Education,* March-April 1960, 141-143.

"Editor's Report, II." *Religious Education*, November-December 1960, 424, 451–452.

1961

"Organization Is Necessary." *Findings*, December 1961, 7–8.
"Christian Insights in Marriage." *The Adult Student*, April 1961, 14–38.
"Protestant Nurture in a Changing World, *Religious Education*, May-June 1961, 199–206.
"The Church in the Bible," *World Christian Education*, First Quarter 1961, 12–14.
"Christian Education in the Church." *World Christian Education*, Second Quarter 1961, 46–49.
"The Parish-wide Program of Christian Education," *World Christian Education*, Third Quarter 1961, 78–81.
"Family and Church and Youth in the Church." *World Christian Education*, Fourth Quarter 1961, 104–107.

1962

"What Should Be the Main Service: Morning Prayer." *The Witness*, Feb. 15, 1962.
"Contemporary Images of Man." *Adult Student* November 1962, 24–44,64.
"The Holy Spirit and Christian Education." *Religious Education*, May-June 1962, 178–184.
"The Holy Spirit and Christian Education." *Biblical Theology* (Belfast), October 1962, 49–63.

1963

"The Holy Spirit and Christian Education." *Findings*, March 1963, 12–14.

1964

"Anxiety and Learning." *Pastoral Psychology*, February 1964, 11–15.
"For the World of Tomorrow." *One Christian Century*, April 29, 1964, 544–546.
"Christian Education as I See It Today." *Baptist Leader*, September 1964, 4–5.
"Children's Questions about Faith." *Adult Student*, November 1964, 2–5.

1965

"New Thinking in Christian Education." *Concordia Theological Monthly*, XXXVI, Feb. 1965, 80–88.
"Resetting Our Sights in Christian Education." *Concordia Theological Monthly*, XXXVI, March 1965, 144–151.
"From Where I Sit." *Religious Education*, March-April 1965, 99–105.
"Moral Behavior for Christians." *Anglican Theological Review*. April 1965.

1966

"The Teaching Ministry." *Navy Supervisory Chaplains Conference*, 17–21 January, 1966, 181–188, 189–192.

"Christian Education in a Secular Society." *Lutheran Education*, September 1966, 2–8.
"Linguistic Models and Religious Education." *Religious Education*, July-August 1966, 269–278.
"The Challenge of the Ecumenical Movement to Church Education." *Religious Education*, September-October 1966, 369–376.

1967

"The Easter Event and Linguistic Analysis: A Critique of Van Buren." *The Near East School of Theology Quarterly*, April and July 1967, 6–21.
"Do We Need an Ordained Ministry?" *The Pulpit*, May 1967, 8–10.
"New Curriculum in Orthodox Churches." *Overseas Mission Review*, XII, No. 3, Whitsunday 1967, 32–34.
"Editor's Report, I." *Religious Education*, May-June 1967, 262–264.
"Editor's Report, II." *Religious Education*, November-December 1967, 466, 536–538.
"Christian Education as a Theological Discipline and Method." *Near East School of Theology Quarterly*, October 1967, 7–16 (cf. Religious Education, November-December 1953).
"Nairobi 1967 Report." *World Christian Education*, Fourth Quarter 1967 (recorder and editor).

1968

"Sprachmodelle und Religionunterricht." *Theologica Practica*, April 1968, 117–130 (Cf. *Religious Education*, July-August 1966, 269–278).
"From Where I Sit." *Learning for Living*, Vo. 7, Nos. 5 & 6, May 1968, 7–9, & September 1968, 22–25.

1969

"How to Use the Bible." *Resource* (Anglican Church of Canada), November 1969, 9–11; December 1969, 5–8.

1970

"How to Use the Bible." *The South-East Asia Journal of Theology*, Vol 11, Spring 1970, 77–82.
"Linguistic Philosophy and Religious Education." *Religious Education*, LXV, No. 4, July-August 1970, 309–317.
"The Language Gap and God," "Religion in State Schools," "Is There a Right Age for Confirmation?" *Christian Education News* (Australia), July 1970, 3–6, 9–12, 13–15.
"Some Asian Contributions to Christian Education." *The South-East Asia Journal of Theology*, Vol 12, Autumn 1970, 3–13.
"Suggested Books for a Christian Education Library." *The South-East Asia Journal of Theology*, Vol 12, Autumn 1970, 48–51.
"Editor's Report I." *Religious Education*, LXV, No. 5, September–October 1970, 386, 447–449.
"Editor's Report II." *Religious Education*, LXV, No. 6, November–December 1970, 466, 517–520.

1971

"Some Asian Contributions to Christian Education." *Religious Education*, LXVI, No 2, March-April 1971, 119-129.
"New Challenges in Religious Education." *National Catholic Reporter*, October 1971.

1972

"Predicaments and Pointers in Religious Education." *Colloquy*, November 1972, 2-5.

1973

"Process Theology and Religious Education." *The St. Luke's Journal of Theology*, March 1973, 3-10.
"A Memory of Ernest Ligon." *Character Potential*, April 1973, 132-133.
"Whitehead and Religious Education." *Religious Education*, May-June 1973, 315-322 (reprinted in John R. McCall, *Dimensions in Religious Education*, CIM Books, 1973)
"How Open a Society?" *Religious Education*, September-October 1973, 564-568.

1975

"Process Thinking and Religious Education." *Anglican Theological Review*, July 1975, 271-288.
"Iris V. Cully." *The Living Light*, Summer 1975, 282-286.

1976

"Empiricism and Process Theology: God Is What God Does." *The Christian Century*, March 24, 1976, 284-287.
"The Heart of Process Thinking: A Critical Overview." *The New Review of Books and Religion*, October, 1976, 6.
"Some Clarifying Thoughts in Religious Education." *The Living Light*, Winter, 1976, 487-498.
"Theology and the Future of Religious Education." *Religious Education*, January-February 1977, 467-60.

PAMPHLETS

1945

"Let's Explore the Philippines. National Council of the Protestant Episcopal Church. 1945, 32 pp.

1961

Christian Insights for Marriage (with Leaders' Guide by Edward D. Staples). Abingdon Press, 1961, 62 pp.

1962

The Educational Mission of the Church. World Council of Christian Education and Sunday School Association, 1962, 55 pp.
The Holy Spirit and Christian Education. Religious Education Committee, Friends General Conference, 1962, 20 pp.

CHURCH SCHOOL CURRICULUM

1945

The Challenge of the Church. Cloister Series, grade 10. Morehouse-Barlow, 1945, rev. ed. 1956.

1957

Revised edition of *Climbers of the Steep Ascent* by Mary Jenness. Cloiser Series, grade 9. Morehouse-Barlow, 1957.

BOOKS

What We Can Believe. Charles Scribner's Sons, 1941, 240 pp.
A Guide for Church School Teachers. Cloister Press, 1943, rev. ed. 1947. 131 pp.
Religion Makes Sense. The Seabury Press, 1950, 308 pp.
The Clue to Christian Education. Charles Scribner's Sons, 1950, 211 pp. (Korean and Japanese translations).
A Symphony of the Christian Year. The Seabury Press, 1954, 230 pp. (A Religious Book Club selection).
Education for Christian Living. Prentice-Hall, 1956, 418 pp., rev. ed., 1963, 462 pp. (Korean and Japanese translations).
Biblical Theology and Christian Education. Charles Scribner's Sons, 1956, 226 pp.
Be Not Anxious. The Seabury Press, 1957, 237 pp.
I Remember Jesus. The Seabury Press, 1958, 96 pp.
Christian Nurture and the Church. Charles Scribner's Sons, 1961, 208 pp. (A Religious Book Club selection). (Korean and Japanese translations).
Your Child's Religion. Doubleday & Company, 1962, 164 pp. (rev. ed., Hawthorn Books, 1975).
Youth Considers Parents as People. Thomas Nelson, 1965, 93 pp.
The Language Gap and God. United Church Press, 1970, 199 pp.
Living with Anxiety. United Church Press, 1971, 190 pp.
Live Until You Die. United Church Press, 1973, 157 pp.
The American Spirit in Theology. United Church Press, 1974, 252 pp.
This We Can Believe. Hawthorn Books, 1976, 200 pp.
Editor: *The Church and Organized Movements.* Harper & Row, 1946, 252 p.
Co-editor, with Henry H. Shires: *Christianity and the Contemporary Scene.* Morehouse-Gorham, 1943, 231 p.

ARTICLES IN BOOKS

"Some Trends in American Theology," in *Christianity and the Contemporary Scene,* ed. Randolph Crump Miller & Henry H. Shires. Morehouse-Gorham, 1943, 1–16.

"Christian Education Today," ibid., 1960, 208.

"The Discovery of Resistance and Resource," in *The Church and Organized Movements*, ed. Randolph Crump Miller. Harper & Row, 1946, 3–25; and Introduction, xii–xvi.

"Authority and Freedom in Doctrine," in *Episcopalians United*, ed. Theodore P. Ferris. Morehouse-Gorham, 1946, 12–36.

"Pastoral Psychology and Christian Education," in *Religion and Human Behavior*, ed. Simon Doniger. Association Press, 1954, 217–233.

"Images of Man and the American Scene," in *What Is the Image of Man?* by Randolph Crump Miller and others. United Church Press, 1959, 1–13. Also Preface, vii–ix.

"Prayer Is an Attitude," in *We Believe in Prayer*, ed. Lawrence M. Brings. Denison & Co., 1958, 180–182.

"Theology and the Understanding of Children," in *The Nature of Man in Theological and Psychological Perspective*. ed. Simon Doniger. Harper & Row, 1962, 142–150.

"Wieman's Theological Empiricism," in *The Empirical Theology of Henry Nelson Wieman*, ed. Robert W. Bretall. New York: The Macmillan Co., 1963, Southern Illinois University Press, 1963, 21–39.

"Relationship Theology," in *The Westminster Dictionary of Christian Education*, ed. Kendig Brubaker Cully. The Westminster Press, 1963, 563–565.

Preface to *The Bible Today*, by Clifford M. Jones. Fortress Press, 1964, 7–10.

Preface to *Youth Considers Sex*, by William E. Hulme. Thomas Nelson, 1965, 7–8.

"The Objective of Christian Education," in *Introduction to Christian Education*, ed. Marvin Taylor. Abingdon Press, 1966, 94–104.

"The Challenge of the Ecumenical Movement to Church Education," in *The Episcopal Church and Education*, ed. Kendig Brubaker Cully. Morehouse-Barlow, 1966, 227–240.

"The Discipline of Theology—Seminary and University," in *Does the Church Know How to Teach?* ed. Kendig Brubaker Cully. The Macmillan Co., 1970, 289–313.

"Predicaments and Pointers in Religious Education," in *A Colloquy on Christian Education*, ed. John H. Westerhoff, III. United Church Press, 1972, 188–196.

Foreword to *China and Maoism Today*, by Theodore T. Y. Yeh. Transcultural Press of the East and West, 1976.

Foreword to *Value Perspectives Today*, by John H. Emling. Fairleigh Dickinson University Press, 1977.

"Continuity and Contrast in the Future of Religious Education," in *The Religious Education We Need*. ed. James Michael Lee. Religious Education Press, 1976.

"Process Thought and Black Theology," in *Black Theology II*, ed. Calvin E. Bruce and William R. Jones. Bucknell University Press, 1976.

CONTRIBUTORS

EWERT H. COUSINS, professor of philosophy, Fordham University.

IRIS V. CULLY, Alexander Campbell Hopkins professor of religious education, Lexington Theological Seminary.

KENDIG BRUBAKER CULLY, editor-in-chief, *The New Review of Books and Religion.*

HOWARD GRIMES, professor of religious education, Perkins School of Theology, Southern Methodist University.

REUEL L. HOWE, director emeritus, Institute of Advanced Pastoral Care.

DAVID R. HUNTER, director of educational programs, Council on Religion and International Affairs.

BOARDMAN W. KATHAN, executive secretary, The Religious Education Association of the United States and Canada.

JAMES MICHAEL LEE, chairman of the department of secondary instruction and educational foundations, University of Alabama at Birmingham.

SARA LITTLE, professor of religious education, Union Theological Seminary (Virginia).

NEELY DIXON McCARTER, dean, Union Theological Seminary (Virginia).

THEODORE A. McCONNELL, editor, Fortress Press.

CHARLES F. MELCHERT, dean and professor of religious education, Presbyterian School of Christian Education.

DONALD E. MILLER, professor of religious education, Bethany Theological Seminary.

ROSEMARY RADFORD RUETHER, Georgia Harkness professor of applied theology, Garrett Evangelical Theological Seminary.

DAVID S. STEWARD, professor of religious education, Pacific School of Religion.

MARGARET S. STEWARD, associate professor of psychology, School of Medicine, University of California (Davis).

INDEX

Date Du

Process and
relationship